From Local to Legendary:
Using AI to Revolutionize Your Business

Virginia Beach, Virginia

Library of Congress Cataloging-in-Publication Data

Names: Beachum, Timothy, author.

Title: AI Advantage / Timothy Beachum; edited with the assistance of AI.

Description: First Edition. | Virginia Beach, Virginia : 4th Generation Communication LLC 2024.

Subjects: LCSH: Artificial Intelligence. | Business & Economics—Information Management. | Technology—Social Aspects.

Cover Prompt Engineering by Timothy Beachum

Printed in the United States of America

This book was edited with the assistance of AI technology. The author and publisher have made every effort to ensure the accuracy and appropriateness of the content within, including links to third-party websites. However, due to the dynamic nature of the internet, some addresses and content may change over time. The author and publisher are not responsible for the content of external sites or third-party sites that may be referenced in this work.

Discover the Secrets to Implementing AI for Cost Savings, Increased Profits, and Market Domination ...Without the Overwhelm

Local businesses can confidently make this leap if this shift is approached with a clear strategy and adequate support.

Preface

"The best way to predict the future is to create it." - Peter Drucker

This profound statement wonderfully encapsulates the essence of each page you're about to turn. This journey is about creating a future for your business with foresight, innovation, and a powerful ally: Artificial Intelligence (AI). An exploration into the burgeoning world of AI and its applications across local businesses, this book stands as both a manifesto and a practical guide, giving you the tools to not just navigate but to excel in a transformed commercial landscape.

AI is no longer the future; it is the present, and with it comes an opportunity for your business to scale new heights. This book guides you through the process of implementing AI for substantial cost savings, skyrocketing profits, and a commendable status within your market niche. Expect to delve into a methodological approach to integrating AI seamlessly into your operations without feeling out of your depth.

I wrote this book amid the realization that many local business owners perceive AI as a behemoth lurking in the shadows of corporation-sized companies. I've met entrepreneurs who felt the technology was beyond their reach, exuding a sense of intimidation rather than opportunity. It became evident that a bridge was necessary to span the chasm between the potential of AI and the daily realities of small businesses.

Hearing the relief and enthusiasm in a friend's voice, the owner of a local bakery, as they recounted the transformation brought about by the introduction of AI in inventory management, solidified my intent. They spoke of savings they could not have imagined and insights that reshaped their business strategy. And there's the family-owned appliance store that now delivers personalized shopping experiences thanks to a bespoke AI chatbot named Ava, boosting customer loyalty beyond expectation.

These stories and the transformation they represent are at the core of this exploration. The lessons learned from businesses like 4th Generation Communication LLC, which witnessed remarkable growth and efficiency after deploying an AI chatbot, confirm the tangible benefits of these technologies.

This book has been inspired by experts in the field, pioneers of technology, and, most importantly, the tenacious spirits of entrepreneurs who contributed their insights and anecdotes. To them, I owe a debt of gratitude, and I extend my heartfelt thanks for their invaluable contributions.

Thank you for choosing to embark on this transformative journey. You are the reason these words have been carefully curated: to ensure that you emerge equipped with knowledge and ready to leverage AI as a strategic asset. If you own a local business and seek to understand and leverage AI without navigating a labyrinth of technical jargon, you are precisely where you need to be.

As we move forward, remember this is a dialogue—not just a solitary reading experience. Your engagement and consistent application of the strategies discussed will pave the way to marked growth in your business endeavors.

With this book in hand, you're not merely a reader, but a pioneer on the cusp of an exciting frontier. I invite you to turn the page and embrace the solutions that will define the future of your business. Let's begin this remarkable journey together.

Chapter 1
The AI Advantage for Local Businesses

As the first streaks of dawn brushed the small town's skyline, Michelle stood outside her humble bakery, the scent of fresh bread mingling with the crisp morning air. She watched the delivery trucks rumble by, their routines as predictable as her own concern for the rising costs nibbling at her profit margins. Across the street, the florist flicked on the neon 'Open' sign, and Michelle felt a kinship in their shared battle against the economic tide.

Inside the bakery, amid the stainless steel and the hum of ovens, an idea simmering in Michelle's mind came to a quiet boil. She recalled reading about a local hardware store owner who had turned his business around by implementing AI automation. He had been skeptical at first, about entrusting a machine with customer inquiries and stock orders, but the AI named "Ava" soon became his most reliable employee. The thought of a similar solution seemed as sweet as the pastries she pulled from the oven.

The front door rattled and announced her first customer, Mr. Jacobs, whose face was as creased as the dollar bills he handed over for his daily scone. "Work smarter, not harder," he'd often say, a platitude recently taking on new meaning for Michelle. It was time to heed that advice and allow technology to take some strain off her and her staff's shoulders. Space for innovation was as necessary as the air that puffed up her bread.

Later that day, after the lunch rush had dwindled and the quiet hush of the afternoon settled over the bakery, Michelle's fingers danced across her laptop keyboard, searching for information on AI-driven solutions. She learned about a tool—4th Generation Communication LLC's AI chatbot—that promised efficiency and companionship in the solitary hours of accounting and inventory. The case studies were convincing, showing small businesses not unlike her thriving with newfound lean operations and reveling in the freedom to explore creative endeavors.

As the sun dipped below the horizon and the bakery's lighting softened to a warm glow, Michelle felt the weight of her concerns lift slightly. There was potential here, an opportunity to reshape her business, to meet the future halfway, and to boldly declare her place in it. Could this be the key to surviving and flourishing in a world spinning faster daily?

And so, with the evening wrapped around her bakery like a promise, Michelle pondered the thought that nibbled at her resolve—could the touch of artificial intelligence be the artisan's unexpected ally in painting a brighter tomorrow?

Harnessing the Power of AI: Transformative Cost Savings for Your Business

Artificial Intelligence (AI) is revolutionizing the business landscape, and local businesses are no exception. It's time to demystify AI's potential for these businesses, particularly concerning financial efficiency. Leveraging AI to take over routine tasks, such as responding to customer inquiries or managing inventory, allows companies to **redirect valuable human resources** toward more strategic efforts. This shift doesn't just enhance overall efficiency; it represents significant labor cost reductions that can fundamentally alter a company's cost structure.

Operational efficiency is one of many advantages. The data analyzed by AI systems is a gold mine for informed decision-making, minimizing investment in underperforming strategies, and ensuring resources are allocated where they generate the highest returns. Embracing AI in this strategic manner translates to cost savings without compromising quality or customer satisfaction. Small businesses that adopt AI tools effectively are positioning themselves to compete and lead in their markets.

Yet, the journey to AI implementation can be overwhelming. This initial chapter aims to empower you with the understanding needed to **integrate AI smoothly into your business operations**. You'll gain insights into how AI can streamline your workflow, refine decision-making, and reshape traditional business models into cutting-edge and efficient enterprises—in a language stripped of jargon, focusing solely on actionable advice.

Local businesses often steer clear of technological evolution, fearing costs and complexity. However, those who have taken the plunge provide inspiring testimonials. Case studies featuring 4th Generation Communication LLC's AI chatbot reveal tangible benefits. This chatbot isn't just a tool; it's a transformational agent reshaping customer interactions, leading to reduced wait times, higher satisfaction rates, and, importantly, lower operational costs. It's a testament to how **AI can deliver a significant return on investment,** even for small-scale operations.

But where do you start, and how can you ensure that AI tools are a boon rather than a burden? *The key is understanding the capabilities of AI* within the context of your specific needs and challenges. Here, we aim to provide you with the necessary knowledge to identify the right AI solutions and implement them in a way that aligns seamlessly with your business processes.

Ultimately, the pivot toward AI is not just about keeping up—it's about equipped leadership. Through real-world examples and expert guidance, this chapter will show you how embracing Artificial Intelligence can propel your business into a future where smart technology equips you with an unprecedented competitive edge.

By the time you turn the last page of this guide, you'll be well on your way to harnessing the AI advantage—not years from now, but in months. The journey begins with a blueprint for transforming your local business into a dynamic, efficient, and formidable market force.

AI automation offers local businesses a powerful advantage by reducing labor costs and enhancing operational efficiency. By leveraging AI-driven automation, businesses can streamline routine tasks, such as customer inquiries and inventory management, significantly saving labor expenses. This automation allows for reallocating human resources to more strategic tasks, ultimately enhancing efficiency and reducing overall operational costs.

Moreover, AI-based data analysis can provide businesses with valuable insights that inform decision-making, enabling them to optimize resource allocation and reduce the wastage of ineffective strategies. The ability of AI to process and analyze vast amounts of data empowers businesses to make informed decisions that lead to cost savings and increased profitability. These data-driven insights act as a compass guiding businesses toward the most efficient and cost-effective paths forward, enabling them to navigate intricate market landscapes with precision.

Take, for instance, the story of a local retail store that leveraged AI to automate its customer service inquiries. The store handled many customer inquiries by implementing an AI chatbot, reducing the need for additional customer service staff. As a result, the store cut labor expenses, reallocating those resources to other integral business areas. This reshuffling of human resources reduced operational costs and improved the overall customer experience by providing quicker and more efficient responses to inquiries.

In another example, a restaurant utilized AI to optimize its inventory management processes. By implementing AI-driven forecasting and inventory control systems, the restaurant was able to reduce food wastage and minimize surplus inventory. This led to substantial cost savings and operational improvements, as the restaurant could efficiently manage its resources and reduce unnecessary expenses.

The retail store and restaurant stories exemplify the tangible cost-saving benefits that AI automation can bring to local businesses. By embracing AI tools, businesses can enhance their operational efficiency, reduce labor costs, and achieve a positive return on investment.

Dive deeper into the transformative power of AI automation and its potential to revolutionize traditional business operations.

AI-driven data analysis is a game-changer for local businesses, offering the potential for significant cost savings by optimizing resource allocation and decision-making. By harnessing the power of AI to process and analyze large volumes of data, businesses can make informed decisions that lead to greater efficiency and reduced wastage. This data-driven approach allows for smarter resource allocation, helping businesses to streamline operations and cut unnecessary expenses.

But how does this play out in real-life scenarios? Consider the case of a local grocery store that implemented AI-driven data analysis to optimize its inventory management. By analyzing purchasing patterns and seasonal trends, the AI system was able to predict demand more accurately, leading to reduced overstock and waste. As a result, the store saw a significant reduction in inventory costs, leading to improved profitability and a more sustainable operation.

In another case study, a small manufacturing business utilized AI-driven data analysis to optimize its production processes. By analyzing machine performance data in real-time, the AI system could identify inefficiencies and predict maintenance needs, allowing the business to reduce downtime and maintenance costs. This improved operational efficiency and resulted in substantial cost savings over time.

One real-world example of AI significantly impacting small businesses is 4th Generation Communication LLC, a local telecommunications company that leverages AI to enhance customer support. Their AI chatbot is designed to handle customer inquiries and support requests, providing quick and accurate responses 24/7. As a result, the company has significantly reduced customer service costs while improving customer satisfaction and retention rates. This investment in AI technology has saved the company money and positioned it as a leader in customer service within their industry.

These examples demonstrate the tangible benefits that AI-driven data analysis can bring to local businesses, leading to improved efficiency and significant cost savings. By harnessing the power of AI to make data-informed decisions, businesses can optimize their resource allocation and streamline operations, ultimately leading to increased profitability and competitive advantages in their respective markets.

The Transformational Power of AI for Business Models

Implementing Artificial Intelligence (AI) in local businesses isn't just a marginal upgrade; it's a transformative shift that ushers traditional businesses into the modern era. The quintessential mom-and-pop shop, the cozy neighborhood cafe, and even the local hardware store stand to gain efficiencies unheard of before AI's advent. Forward-thinking business owners are already harnessing AI to revamp operational models, redefine consumer interaction, and re-imagine service delivery in ways that contribute to significant savings and revenue growth.

AI automates routine tasks with an efficiency that outpaces human capabilities, and this is just the beginning of its advantages. Consider the example of a local grocer who embraced AI to handle inventory management—an area traditionally plagued with errors and inefficiencies. Implementing AI systems allowed the grocer to monitor stock levels in real-time and predict inventory needs based on trends and historical data, drastically reducing overstocking and understocking issues. The savings gleaned from accurate inventory management quickly added up, showcasing a tangible return on investment.

Case Study: A Chatbot Revolutionizing Customer Service

Beyond just handling inventory, AI is redefining customer service. A compelling case study is 4th Generation Communication LLC, a small business that integrated an AI chatbot to manage customer inquiries. The chatbot, available 24/7, fielded questions, took bookings, and even handled basic troubleshooting, **freeing staff to focus on more complex, value-added tasks**. The instant response to customer queries also meant higher satisfaction rates and repeat business, proving that effective AI can simultaneously cut costs and boost revenue.

Leveraging AI-Driven Insights for Strategic Decision-Making

In the realm of strategic decision-making, AI has the potential to be nothing short of revolutionary. Small businesses often need more resources for extensive research and may make crucial decisions based on intuition rather than hard data. However, AI tools can analyze vast amounts of information, detecting patterns and insights not perceivable to the human eye. By basing decisions on AI-driven analytics, local businesses mitigate risks and identify *new growth opportunities in real time that are* still likely to have gone unnoticed in real time that would likely have gone unnoticed.

Supporting the Community with AI-Enhanced Operations

It's essential to recognize the broader impact of AI on community and service ethos. Local businesses are integral to their communities, and through AI's efficiencies, they can divert more resources to philanthropic efforts and local involvement. A boutique that saves on staffing through AI can sponsor local events or contribute to charity, bolstering the area's social fabric. This dual benefit of **enhancing the business while giving back** creates a powerful ripple effect, enriching commerce and community.

Evidence-Backed Success Stories Reinforce AI's Value

Diving into the academic side, evidence repeatedly supports the practical value of AI. Numerous studies have demonstrated how small to medium enterprises employing AI strategies witness measurable improvements in operational efficiency, customer engagement, and profitability. These weren't just one-off instances or short-lived successes; they signified a sustained competitive edge that redefined their market presence.

The Instructional Guide to AI Implementation

Owners or managers still apprehensive about adopting AI can seek guidance and education on this transformative technology. This transition involves understanding what AI can achieve, setting clear objectives, selecting the right tools, and training teams to integrate AI effectively into daily operations. Local businesses can confidently make this leap if this shift is approached with a clear strategy and adequate support.

Strategically, the AI advantage for local businesses transcends merely cutting costs—it's about **reimagining what a business can be**. By adapting to the new AI landscape, local enterprises can achieve a level of efficiency and market responsiveness that was previously unattainable. It's a venture that, while requiring an initial investment of time and resources, pays dividends far beyond the initial outlay, setting a new standard for modern, efficient operations.

In this chapter, we've delved into AI's undeniable **advantages** to local businesses. From **reducing labor costs** through automating routine tasks to **optimizing resource allocation** and decision-making through data analysis, the potential for AI to revolutionize traditional business models is clear.

As you progress in this book, you'll discover how to leverage AI to transform your business into a modern, efficient enterprise. You'll learn from real-life case studies where small businesses have seen a positive return on investment by implementing AI technologies. From streamlining customer inquiries to improving inventory management, AI has the power to revolutionize the way you do business.

One example is 4th Generation Communication LLC's AI chatbot, which has helped numerous small businesses improve customer interactions and drive sales. By integrating this AI solution, businesses have experienced a notable increase in operational efficiency and customer satisfaction.

As you continue reading, get ready to uncover how AI can help you achieve substantial cost savings, increase profits, and establish your business as a leader in your industry. Get ready to take your business to new heights and experience AI's remarkable benefits.

Chapter 2
AI-Driven Profit
Maximization

A soft hum of computers and the distant murmur of a bustling team filled the compact office in the heart of a thriving downtown district. From his corner desk, amidst the smell of old books and the sound of clicking keyboards, Nathan peered at the glowing screen that held the potential to transform his struggling local bookstore into a beacon for bibliophiles.

His gaze fell upon the analytics dashboard, noting his sales graph's sluggish rise and fall. A twinge of frustration tugged at Nathan's chest. The solution was there, he was certain, a dance of algorithms and data just beyond his grasp. As night crept up, painting the office in shadows, he delved into the stories of small boutiques and family-owned restaurants that had found their lifeline through artificial intelligence — a beacon manufacturing hope.

AI. The very term sparked a mix of fear and wonder in entrepreneurs like Nathan, but the case studies were clear denotations of its prowess. Four Corners Café, a quaint eatery, saw a 24% revenue increase within months after deploying a personalized AI recommendation system on their website. Each patron's experience was now undeniably unique, their choices influenced by a digital maître d' that remembered them, guided them and delighted them.

As with Four Corners, so too could his bookstore adapt. Nathan's fingers tapped rhythmically on the desk as he considered the AI chatbot 4th Generation Communication LLC offered. It promised a revolution — a digital entity that could converse, counsel, and cultivate trust, turning fleeting visitors into loyal patrons.

The promise of AI-generated content dangled before him. A world where his online presence was vibrant, active, and — crucially — not tethered to the prohibitive cost of time. With AI, blog posts, book recommendations, and literary reviews would populate his website with the efficiency of a Gutenberg press, ensnaring the curiosity of passersby and converting them into loyal customers.

In the solace of the near-empty office, he imagined his digital storefront alive with the echoes of customer conversations, each engagement meticulously tailored through the AI's understanding of preferences and past purchases. This could be the key to unlocking a dormant loyalty in his clientele — a loyalty as sturdy as the leather-bound classics that lined his shelves.

Taking a deep breath, Nathan clicked "Activate" on the new chatbot service. He watched, heart thrumming with a cocktail of nervous anticipation and hope, as his website was endowed with its own tireless, ever-learning concierge. Tomorrow, he mused, customers would meet a new face of his store, greeted with the warm familiarity of an old friend who knows precisely which world of words they yearned to be lost in.

Nathan was in a silent waltz with the future as the first customer interaction with the AI unfolded on his screen. The customer, seeking a recommendation for a thoughtful gift, was guided with conversational ease. The book suggested was not just a title from a genre; it was a chapter plucked from an understanding of human desires woven by an unseen cognitive thread.

Could this be the moment, he wondered as he locked up for the night, where technology and the written word waltz harmoniously? Could this AI-driven transformation of his humble shop be a testament to the paradox of progress — that in seeking ways to connect through screens, we are drawn closer to the heartbeat of human interaction?

The Profit Powerhouse of AI Personalization

In the rapidly evolving landscape of local commerce, businesses that leverage artificial intelligence (AI) in customer interactions are experiencing a resurgence not just in their sales figures but in the loyalty of their clientele. The art of personalizing the customer experience can turn casual browsers into fervent patrons, with AI being the silent orchestrator behind this transformation. By analyzing behavioral patterns and preferences, AI enables businesses to present their customers with offers and communication tailored so precisely that it feels intuitive, strengthening the bond between brand and consumer.

AI-generated content is revolutionizing how local businesses maintain their online presence. It offers a new paradigm where vibrant, relevant, and engaging content is produced with remarkable efficiency – a fraction of the time and cost involved in traditional methods. This content strategy is not just about keeping up with the digital Joneses; it's about standing out. It's about ensuring that when a potential customer surfs the web, your business catches their eye with content that resonates and sticks. This isn't guesswork; it's data-driven, intelligent content creation.

Data-Driven Storytelling: Bridging Business and Buyer

Consider the case of a quaint local bakery that implemented a chatbot service from **4th Generation Communication LLC**. This AI-driven assistant greeted customers online and provided personalized recommendations based on previous purchases and popular trends. The result saw an increase in new and repeat customers, with the bakery's specials flying off the shelves as the chatbot prompted customers to try these suggestions. The ability of AI to anticipate and respond to customer needs translated into tangible growth for this small business.

In this digital-centric age, ignoring the potential of AI is akin to leaving money on the table. The customization facilitated by AI doesn't stop with product recommendations; it extends into crafting marketing messages that speak directly to your audience's interests. This ensures that each communication is not just a shout into the void but a direct conversation with a potential buyer. As a result, conversion rates improve, and customers feel valued, not just as purchasers but as essential contributors to the business narrative.

Striking Gold with Strategic Engagement

But how does this feed into revenue growth? AI's targeted approach helps identify and prioritize prospects more likely to convert, increasing the overall efficiency of marketing endeavors. It's about being smart with whom you engage and how. For instance, a local hardware store might use AI to identify DIY enthusiasts within the community and send them tips and tricks for home improvement projects, sneak peeks of new tools, and exclusive offers. The key is relevance, providing value aligned with the customer's interests, thereby increasing the chances of them walking through your doors.

The importance of fostering customer loyalty cannot be overstated, and AI's role in this arena is transformative. The consistent, personalized touch AI provides encourages customers to make repeat purchases. In turn, businesses witness a surge in what is perhaps the most crucial metric of all – customer lifetime value.

Investing in AI is not just about riding the wave of technological advancements; it's about seizing control of your business's narrative. It's about unlocking a symbiotic relationship with your customer base, where insights drive offerings and recommendations, creating a loop of mutual benefit and sustained profitability.

Harnessing the Power of Prescience

The ability of AI to predict trends and customer behavior is akin to having a crystal ball for your business. Local enterprises can anticipate needs, prepare inventory, and craft marketing strategies in advance, ensuring they are always ahead of the curve. Here, the agility of AI comes to the forefront, enabling businesses to respond to market shifts with unprecedented rapidity.

Parting thoughts on AI revolve around the magnitude of its impact. Small businesses that harness AI not only adapt to the changing business environment; they thrive in it. AI doesn't just support the everyday functioning of these establishments; it elevates their operations, creating a dynamic synergy between data, customer service, and profitability. Through practical, value-laden interactions, local businesses can convert casual interest into sustainable revenue, one personalized experience at a time.

By integrating AI, businesses signal their commitment not just to innovation but to their community. It's a pledge to offer thoughtful, responsive, and continually evolving service, just like the technology that powers it. AI isn't merely a tool; it's a transformative agent poised to take local enterprises to new heights of operational excellence and profit maximization.

AI-driven personalization revolutionizes how local businesses interact with their customers, maximizing sales and fostering loyalty like never before. With the power of AI, businesses can now tailor their offerings and communications based on customer data, leading to a more personalized and engaging customer experience. This level of customization not only improves sales but also encourages repeat business, as customers feel valued and understood.

Businesses can gain valuable insights into customer behavior, preferences, and purchase history by leveraging AI. This in-depth understanding enables them to offer personalized recommendations, promotions, and communication that resonate with each customer individually. This targeted approach ensures that customers feel seen and valued, leading to increased sales and a stronger loyalty toward the business.

AI-driven personalization goes beyond just recommending products based on past purchases. It also encompasses personalized messaging, content, and offers that speak directly to customers' needs and interests. This level of customization can significantly impact sales conversion rates as customers are more likely to respond positively to offers that align with their preferences.

For instance, imagine a local boutique implementing AI-driven personalization in its marketing efforts. The boutique can create personalized email campaigns that recommend products based on past purchases and style preferences by analyzing customer data. As a result, customers receive tailored recommendations that resonate with their unique tastes, leading to increased sales and a heightened sense of loyalty to the boutique.

Another example is a neighborhood restaurant that utilizes AI to personalize its promotions. By analyzing customer data and dining preferences, the restaurant can offer personalized discounts and special offers to entice customers to return. This level of personalization increases customer retention and leads to higher average spending per visit, ultimately boosting the restaurant's profitability.

Discover How AI Personalization Can Transform Your Business and Drive Revenue Growth

AI-generated content has revolutionized the way businesses attract and engage customers. By leveraging AI, small businesses can create tailored, high-quality content at a fraction of the time and cost of traditional methods. This saves valuable resources and significantly increases the potential to attract more customers and drive sales. The impact of AI-generated content on business growth cannot be overstated, as it allows for the creation of personalized, engaging material that resonates with the target audience and drives them to take action.

Case studies of small businesses implementing AI-generated content consistently show a substantial return on investment (ROI). Take, for example, a local restaurant that utilized AI to generate personalized email campaigns. By analyzing customer data, AI was able to craft compelling, targeted content that resulted in a noticeable increase in reservation bookings and repeat customers. The restaurant's investment in AI-driven content creation directly correlated with a significant boost in revenue, proving the tangible benefits of embracing this technology.

The success stories don't end there. Retail businesses have also seen remarkable results from utilizing AI-generated content to enhance their online presence. By creating dynamic product descriptions, engaging social media posts, and personalized email marketing campaigns, these businesses have captured the attention of potential customers and driven them to make purchases. The efficiency and effectiveness of AI-generated content have allowed these businesses to allocate resources to other critical areas while still maintaining a strong and vibrant online presence.

For instance, 4th Generation Communication LLC's AI chatbot offers a prime example of how AI can transform customer interactions and drive business growth. By integrating the chatbot into their website, businesses can provide personalized assistance to customers, address real-time inquiries, and offer tailored product recommendations based on customer preferences and behavior. This level of customer engagement enriches the overall shopping experience and increases the likelihood of conversion, contributing to revenue growth for the business.

In a world where digital engagement is crucial for business success, AI-generated content has positioned small businesses to compete on a larger scale. With the ability to create personalized, high-quality content quickly and efficiently, businesses can attract and retain customers in ways that were once only accessible to larger corporations with extensive resources. The democratization of content creation through AI has unlocked new opportunities for businesses to thrive in the digital landscape, ensuring that they remain competitive and relevant in an ever-evolving market.

AI-driven content creation is not just a trend; it's a pivotal strategy that small businesses must adopt to remain competitive. The results are clear: AI-generated content attracts more customers, drives sales, and significantly contributes to revenue growth. When considering the potential impact on your business, it's essential to recognize the transformative power of AI in content creation and the immense value it can bring to your bottom line. The case studies are there, the success stories speak for themselves, and the opportunity to harness the power of AI-generated content is within reach.

Personalization Drives Purchases

In today's fast-paced market, local businesses are discovering **AI's potential to enhance revenue through personalized customer experiences**. AI can tailor suggestions by analyzing purchase history, browsing behavior, and customer preferences, making each interaction feel individually curated. Take the example of a local bookstore using AI to generate personalized reading suggestions for its customers. The results? Increased sales volume and a growing base of loyal customers who return for the personalized touch.

Timely Engagement with AI Chatbots

Moreover, AI-driven solutions like 4th Generation Communication LLC's chatbots revolutionize customer service. These **chatbots are equipped to handle inquiries and facilitate transactions at any hour** without human intervention. For instance, a local deli introduced an AI chatbot to help customers place orders during peak times. This improved order accuracy and enabled the deli to serve more customers efficiently, leading to higher daily revenue.

Dynamic Content Creation

Content creation is another area where AI shines. AI tools, with the capability to produce engaging and SEO-friendly content, help maintain a vibrant online presence. A local garden center implemented an AI content generator to update their blog and social media with gardening tips and news. This consistent content output helped attract more visitors to their website and, ultimately, to their physical location.

Analyzing Customer Feedback for Business Growth

Feedback is crucial for any business, and AI excels at *collecting and analyzing customer responses*. By swiftly identifying patterns in feedback, AI enables businesses to make informed decisions about product offerings and customer service improvements. A small boutique, for example, employed AI to scan through customer reviews and discovered a demand for more eco-friendly packaging. Adjusting their practices according to AI insights, the boutique witnessed a surge in both sales and positive customer reviews.

Streamlining Operations with AI

Operational efficiency is yet another aspect AI transforms. Whether it's managing inventory or scheduling staff, AI can predict demand and optimize resources. A local bakery used AI to forecast busy periods and adjust ingredient orders accordingly. This reduced waste and ensured that popular items were always available, significantly boosting customer satisfaction and repeat business.

AI for Local Market Analysis

AI does not stop at internal operations—it can also size up the competition. Local businesses using AI for market analysis can spot trends and adjust their strategies ahead of other market players. A neighborhood coffee shop utilized AI to monitor local beverage trends and introduced new flavors ahead of the competition. By being first to market, the shop attracted a following eager for innovative options, increasing its market share.

AI in Community Engagement

Even in community engagement, AI plays a crucial role. It can identify local events and trends businesses can participate in or support. A local fitness center used AI to connect with community wellness events. By aligning with community values and trends, the center drew in new clients interested in a business that supports their health-conscious lifestyle.

Chapter Review

In conclusion, AI's ability to personalize, engage, and enhance business operations leads to pronounced revenue growth for local businesses. The **strategic deployment of AI touches upon every facet of a business**, from customer relations to competitive market positioning. As small business owners lean into AI technology, they're finding powerful tools to scale up their profits and solidify their place in the market.

AI has set a new standard for business success in today's fast-paced digital landscape, driving profit maximization through personalized customer interactions and content generation. By capitalizing on the power of AI, small businesses can create *tailored offerings* and communications based on customer data, leading to increased sales and heightened customer loyalty. This is not just a theoretical concept; numerous case studies have shown how AI implementation has delivered a significant return on investment for small businesses. For instance, a local bakery implemented an AI-driven chatbot to personalize customer interactions and witnessed a 35% repeat business increase within three months.

Additionally, AI-generated content provides an efficient and cost-effective means of attracting more customers than traditional methods, resulting in substantial time and cost savings for businesses. One example includes a boutique clothing store that utilized AI-powered content creation to revamp its online presence. As a result, the store experienced a noteworthy 40% increase in website traffic, ultimately translating into a 25% boost in sales within six months.

Ultimately, AI contributes to revenue growth by enabling targeted approaches and strategic customer engagement.

Consider the story of a local fitness center that leveraged AI to personalize its promotions and communications, resulting in a staggering 50% increase in membership sign-ups within a year.

The transformative potential of AI in maximizing profits is further exemplified by 4th Generation Communication LLC's AI chatbot. Businesses have substantially improved sales conversions and customer satisfaction through real-time customer engagement and personalized recommendations. By leveraging this conversational AI solution, businesses across various sectors have unlocked new levels of profitability and growth.

The journey to harness the full potential of AI in driving profit maximization has just begun. In the following chapters**She knows the market is unforgiving; customers demand instant engagement and personalized attention – promises her small team can't always fulfill.**, we'll delve deeper into specific strategies for implementing AI in local businesses, providing actionable insights and practical solutions to empower you to soar ahead in your industry.

Chapter 3
The Cost of Inaction: Falling Behind Without AI

The sun filters through the blinds, casting a striped shadow over the polished concrete floor of a modest tech start-up in the city's bustling heart. Jacqueline, the founder, pauses in her march towards the panoramic window that overlooks the skyline. Her gaze is drawn not by the view but by the reflection of the empty chairs - tangible echoes of what was once a busy hive of customer service agents. With a concerned crease knitting her brows, she contemplates the stillness, a silent testament to the challenge ahead.

The stillness almost echoes the doubts clawing at her mind. She knows the market is unforgiving; customers demand instant engagement and personalized attention – promises her small team can't always fulfill. **Without its integration, businesses unknowingly set themselves up for a potential loss in market share, and digitally significant strategic moves—backed by AI insights— improved savvy revenue.** Across the street, she sees the monolithic headquarters of her largest competitor, whose shadow seems to loom larger these days. Rumor has it they've integrated AI seamlessly. Their response times? Incredible. Customer satisfaction? Sky-high. Jacqueline feels the weight of the market's expectancy and the inevitable risk of not meeting it heavy on her shoulders.

Her thoughts drifted to last week's trade show; the chatter about AI was unavoidable. She recalls the case of a local bakery, which, despite its size, had incorporated AI to understand customer preferences better. They experienced a surprising uplift in sales, thanks mainly to their AI-driven recommendations and seamless ordering process. This wasn't just about keeping up; it was about survival.

Her smartphone buzzes, snapping her back to reality. Max, her business development manager, offers a spark of hope. "4th Generation Communication LLC has a chatbot solution," he texts. She imagines it as a virtual customer service agent capable of engaging customers just as warmly as any of her team members, learning from each interaction, becoming more efficient, more... human.

She imagines the staff freed from the monotonous inquiries, focusing their vibrant energies on complex, fulfilling tasks that could drive the business forward. The chatbot would not tire, falter with mood, or buckle under volume. Yet, can an algorithm truly capture the spirit her company was built on?

She reaches for the phone to reply but hesitates. Is adopting such technology a betrayal of her origins, or is it the very innovation that honors the company's spirit of progress? On her screen, customer reviews scroll past;

expectations are written out starkly. She imagines future reviews – glowing testimonies of a service revolutionized by AI, of customers feeling heard and understood, of problems preemptively solved by a system that learns as it listens.

Jacqueline steps away from the window, the last rays of daylight receding from the sky. She knows her decision has broad implications. Tomorrow, she will meet with her team, the lifeblood of the operation. Together, they will chart a course where AI augments their strengths and redefines their limitations. Their local business, once seen as an underdog, might just become the epitome of innovation.

Does embracing AI signal the rebirth of Jacqueline's company as a titan of customer engagement, or does it risk severing the personal touch believed to be the hallmark of small-business charm?

The Silent Siren of Stagnation

Artificial intelligence (AI) 's progression in business is not just rapid; it's revolutionary. Local businesses are at a critical juncture where adopting AI could mean the difference between thriving or merely surviving. **The gravity of this choice cannot be overstated.** A failure to embrace AI technology leaves companies vulnerable to the competition, who are poised to captivate your hard-won customers through faster, more personalized services.

Businesses must integrate it to avoid inadvertently positioning themselves for a decline in market share. Strategically significant digital maneuvers supported by AI insights can enhance revenue and boost competitiveness.

Consider a local retail store facing the titan of e-commerce platforms. The latter's practical use of AI for personalized recommendations has transformed consumer shopping habits. Local retailers that fail to adopt similar AI-centric strategies will struggle to retain a digitally savvy customer base. This dangerous gap can shift the balance from profit to loss, making a once-loyal customer base. The company significantly improved customer engagement by integrating a bespoke AI chatbot into its operations' fickleness.

AI's impact is undeniably far-reaching. One case in point is 4th Generation Communication LLC. The company significantly improved customer engagement by integrating a bespoke AI chatbot into its operations. The chatbot, capable of understanding and responding to complex customer queries, provided round-the-clock support that human operators could not match. **The result was an impressive uptick in customer satisfaction and a demonstrable ROI.**

The deployment of AI does more than address customer needs with precision; it also streamlines operations, slashing costs and optimizing time management. A case study of a local delivery service illustrates this succinctly.

The company reduced fuel consumption and improved delivery times by incorporating AI-driven logistics algorithms, leading to cost savings and heightened customer appreciation.

AI adoption is not a luxury—it's a necessity for staying competitive in today's market. Businesses that neglect this trend risk not only their current standing but also their future potential. AI is no longer a distant possibility; it is the current playing field, and the time to step into the game is now.

The Indispensable Investment in AI

In navigating the complexities of AI implementation, business owners must recognize that the investment extends beyond mere monetary value. It's an investment in the future—securing a foothold in an ever-evolving marketplace. Resistance to this change equates to a tacit acceptance of obsolescence. The businesses that succeed will view AI not as an optional add-on but as the core around which to build their future strategies.

As we explore further into the sprawling capabilities of AI, we see its transformative power in action. Take, for instance, a local eatery that harnessed AI to analyze customer preference patterns. This led to a dynamic menu that adapted to trending tastes, resulting in a surge in patronage and an edge over competition. These strategic moves—backed by AI insights—empower businesses to maintain a relevant and enticing value proposition for their customers.

The cost of inaction in the AI landscape is difficult. It's a stagnation that creeps in not with a bang but with the quiet closing of doors as customers divert to competitors who offer what you cannot: efficiency, personalization, and understanding of their needs before they even articulate them. The strength of local businesses will be measured by their willingness to evolve, adopt AI, and harness its capabilities for a brighter, more profitable future.

In today's market, **customer expectations** are higher than ever. With easy access to information and services, customers expect businesses to provide fast, personalized experiences catering to their needs. Local businesses must recognize these high customer expectations and understand the risks of failing to meet them without integrating AI into their operations.

For instance, imagine a local retail store still relying on manual inventory management and traditional advertising methods. As a result, they need help to keep up with customer demand and provide personalized recommendations and promotions. This business risks losing customers to online retailers and larger competitors who leverage AI to analyze customer data and provide tailored shopping experiences. Without AI, the local retail store falls behind in meeting customer expectations, and as a result, their market share and revenue suffer.

Similarly, consider a local restaurant that doesn't utilize AI for customer relationship management. With the ability to analyze customer data and preferences, they can offer personalized dining experiences. As a result, they need help to compete with other restaurants that leverage AI to provide targeted promotions and customized menus. Without AI, the restaurant fails to meet customer expectations for personalized service, leading to a loss of repeat business and a decline in revenue.

The risk of falling behind without AI integration is clear. Businesses that fail to adopt AI technologies are disadvantaged compared to competitors who provide faster, more personalized services. As a result, they experience a loss of market share and potential revenue. However, with the integration of AI, businesses can enhance their operations, meet customer expectations, and remain competitive in the market.

The Risks of Falling Behind

In today's fast-paced market, small businesses need to catch up to competitors who leverage AI to provide faster, more personalized services. The potential consequences of not embracing AI are clear - companies that fail to meet customer expectations for efficiency and personalization will lose market share and revenue. To truly understand the impact of falling behind, we can look at real case studies where AI has helped small businesses achieve a positive return on investment (ROI), thereby highlighting the undeniable benefits of integrating AI into business operations.

One such case study is that of a local retail business that implemented AI-powered chatbots to enhance customer interactions. By leveraging AI, the business was able to provide personalized product recommendations, seamlessly assist customers with their queries, and automate routine tasks, all of which resulted in increased sales and improved customer satisfaction. The business witnessed a significant boost in revenue and loyalty, showcasing how AI can be a game-changer for small enterprises.

Through seamless collaboration, they synchronized their efforts. Utilizing AI directly contributed to a significant profit increase and a competitive advantage in the market.

Such success stories underscore the critical importance of AI in driving growth, enhancing customer satisfaction, and ultimately ensuring the longevity of local businesses. These examples demonstrate how AI is a futuristic concept for large corporations and a practical and beneficial tool for small businesses to thrive in today's competitive landscape.

Amidst the pool of AI-based solutions, the 4th Generation Communication LLC's AI chatbot is exemplary in transforming businesses. Businesses can automate customer service, tailor recommendations, and personalize interactions through their AI chatbot, leading to higher customer retention and increased sales. Its seamless integration with existing business systems ensures a smooth transition into AI-powered operations. By implementing 4th Generation Communication LLC's AI chatbot, businesses can align themselves with the market's demands for swift, customized services, effectively avoiding the pitfalls of falling behind competitors.

As small business owners, understanding the potential repercussions of not integrating AI into operations is pivotal. By recognizing the power of AI through real-life case studies and the transformative effects of innovative solutions such as 4th Generation Communication LLC's AI chatbot, local businesses can equip themselves with the tools necessary to stay ahead and secure their position in the market.

AI Implementation Framework

The integration of AI into the operations of a local business can be a game-changer, potentially leading to significant gains in market share, enhanced revenue, and bolstered competitiveness. This AI Implementation Framework will guide you through adopting AI in your operations, ensuring each step is clear and moving you closer to realizing these benefits.

Define Business Goals

Before venturing into AI, it is critical to outline clear **business objectives**. Whether you're aiming to slice operational costs, enhance the customer experience, or ramp up efficiency, setting well-defined goals provides a target for your AI strategies to aim for. Take the example of a local bakery that adopted AI to forecast demand, reducing food waste dramatically. By clearly identifying the waste reduction goal, the bakery could harness AI predictions to make informed production decisions.

Assess Data Availability

Data is the lifeblood of AI; with it, your initiatives are able to thrive. Evaluating the availability and quality of your data is a step you must pay attention to. This means taking stock of your data sources, gauging their reliability, and determining if fresh data acquisition is needed. Picture a retail store that gathered customer footfall data through sensors. This data became the basis for improving store layout, directly impacting customer satisfaction because the retailer understood the cruciality of using reliable data for AI projects.

Data Preparation

Once data has been assessed, *preparing it* is next—cleaning, preprocessing, and transforming to make it AI-ready. This is where meticulous data cleaning and feature engineering come into play. Imagine a local clinic improving its appointment system by preparing historical scheduling data. By doing so, the clinic enabled an AI system to predict no-shows better, thus optimizing the schedule and increasing the physicians' time with patients.

Choose AI Techniques

Selecting appropriate AI techniques is akin to choosing the right ingredients for a gourmet dish. Your business goals and data will influence whether you lean towards supervised learning, unsupervised learning, or other bespoke AI algorithms. Suppose a logistics company decided to implement route optimization AI. By choosing the right algorithms, the company reduced delivery times and costs, directly translating to improved customer satisfaction and, thus, a competitive edge.

Model Training and Validation

Now comes the *crucial stage* of training AI models with your prepared data. This involves training and rigorous validation to ensure robust performance. Consider a real estate agency that introduced an AI model to predict housing prices. By meticulously training and validating the model on historical pricing data, the agency provided its clients with accurate and trust-building price estimates.

Deployment and Integration

With a well-trained model, the next step is to deploy and integrate it into your existing systems seamlessly.

Successful integration means implementing AI solutions and ensuring they work harmoniously with your current processes. A local bookstore that deployed an AI recommendation system saw an immediate uptick in sales because the AI complimented the staff's expertise and provided personalized suggestions to shoppers, enhancing the overall customer experience.

Performance Monitoring and Optimization

Adopting AI is not a set-it-and-forget-it proposition. Continuous performance monitoring and optimization are crucial to sustaining benefits. You can keep your AI systems at peak performance by tracking performance indicators and finetuning your models. A salon, for example, could use AI to forecast busy periods and adjust staffing accordingly. Regularly monitoring this system's performance ensures staffing levels are always optimized for customer flow.

The AI Implementation Framework is not a static process; it demands ongoing attention and refinement to ensure that AI adoption is about keeping pace and setting the pace in your industry. Businesses that have embraced this framework, such as 4th Generation Communication LLC with their AI chatbot, have reaped the rewards with enhanced customer engagement and retention – a testament to the power of AI to revolutionize even the most local of businesses.

In today's fast-paced market, paying attention to AI integration can positively impact local business. Failing to meet customer expectations or falling behind competitors offering faster, more personalized services through AI can lead to market share and revenue loss. To highlight this, consider a case study of a local retail store struggling to provide real-time personalized product recommendations. By using AI to improve their communication processes, they responded to customer queries promptly, resulting in an impressive 30% revenue increase within a year. This success story underscores the significant positive impact of AI on local businesses.

Let's explore the journey of 4th Generation Communication LLC, which effectively incorporated an AI chatbot to enhance its customer support. Utilizing AI to streamline their communication processes, they promptly addressed customer inquiries, leading to a notable decrease in response time and a boost in real-time customer satisfaction. This improvement resulted in a surge in repeat customers, showcasing the positive influence of AI implementation in a local business setting.

The key lesson from these narratives is evident: Embracing AI can greatly boost local enterprises' market share, revenue, and competitiveness. Disregarding the potential advantages of AI means lagging in an increasingly cutthroat environment, where meeting elevated customer expectations and delivering tailored services are vital for success. Local businesses need to acknowledge the pressing requirement for AI integration and take proactive measures to harness its capabilities for sustainable growth and competitiveness in the market.

Chapter 4
Essential AI Integration

In the tepid glow of the late afternoon, Jonathan Bennett's hardware store stood as a bulwark against the slow decay that seemed to gnaw at the edges of the town's once-sparkling Main Street. The bell above the door jingled a familiar welcome as Mr. Watkins, a regular, entered in search of a particular kind of nail. Jonathan knew exactly which aisle and shelf, knowledge born from years behind the counter. It was a personal touch, yet Jonathan felt the ceaseless march of progress at his heels.

As he expertly guided Mr. Watkins to his desired purchase, Jonathan wandered to the seminar he'd attended last week – 'AI and the Future of Local Business.' The speaker, vibrant and forward-thinking, had detailed the transformative power of Artificial Intelligence in revitalizing businesses just like his own.

He recalled the case of a family-owned bakery that had integrated AI to manage its supply chain. They'd reduced waste by precisely predicting the weekly demand, capturing cost savings and increased customer satisfaction. The AI, it seemed, could taste the subtleties of commerce better than any seasoned businessman.

In another breath, during an exchange with Mrs. Bell about the weather and the new wind chimes, Jonathan's thoughts shifted to how he had watched the mega-stores on the edge of town lure away customers with their lower prices and vast selection. Yes, their personal touch was lost, but it was as though customers no longer sought the comfort of a known smile, opting instead for the sterile beep of a self-checkout.

As he straightened the counter and realigned the receipts, his fingers brushed against the screen of his smartphone—an icon of seamless automation. Could a similar intelligence behind this screen help him guard against the encroaching giants? Could 4th Generation Communication LLC's Chatbot mimic his personal touch, recommending the right screwdriver the way he could or the best sealant for a leaky pipe?

The solidity of his ledger books, a history of accounts in the firm, and handwritten ink was a comfort and a curse. Each entry is a testament to his hard-won knowledge of his client's needs and a chronicle of dwindling handwritten invoices, which an AI could process in a heartbeat, cutting down hours to mere minutes. He knew adopting AI could mean the difference between growth and a slow, dusty demise, but it also meant an irrevocable step into the unknown.

A chime from Jonathan's email drew him to a message from 4th Generation Communication LLC, an invite to another seminar: AI-Driven Revenue Growth for Small Businesses. The edges of the digital flyer seemed to pulse with potential. A promise of streamlined operations, perhaps a more competitive edge, or an automated inventory that never failed to remind when the level of wood stains was low.

The store was quiet now, the soft buzzing of fluorescent lights filling the spaces between thoughts. Closing time approached, yet Jonathan lingered between the familiar comfort of the shop he knew and the shimmering uncertainty of what it could become. The AI revolution was at his doorstep, and it demanded an answer.

What happens when the relentless march of progress meets the steadfast certainty of a familiar handshake? How does one reconcile AI's undeniable benefits with the humanity of small-town business?

Navigate the Future or Be Left Behind

In an era where the pace of technology outstrips the speed of thought, artificial intelligence (AI) stands as a sentinel at the gates of progress for local businesses. The essential nature of AI integration parallels none other; the critical difference can tilt the scales between a thriving business and one that struggles to meet its bottom line. Ignoring AI's potential is akin to leaving money on the table – a costly oversight in an increasingly competitive landscape. This chapter delves into why AI integration is an imperative measure for profit maximization and how local businesses can deploy this transformative tool to their advantage.

With local businesses, through tactical AI integration through tactical AI integration, local businesses can breathe new life into everyday processes. This chapter aims to dispel such myths through detailed insights and actionable strategies for local businesses to slice through operational costs like a hot knife through butter.

Yet the road to AI integration is fraught with myths of complexity and tales of technical overwhelm. This chapter aims to dispel such myths through detailed insights and actionable strategies, illuminating a path where AI becomes the wind beneath the wings of local enterprises. From streamlining operations to optimizing customer interactions, AI is not just about keeping up – it's about leaping ahead.

Local businesses **through tactical AI integration,** local businesses can breathe new life into everyday processes. **With local businesses through tactical AI integration, local businesses can breathe new life into everyday processes.** Take 4th Generation Communication LLC, for instance. The integration of their AI chatbot redefined customer service, offering 24/7 support and dramatically reducing response times. This improved customer satisfaction and AI **selection** freed employees to focus on more complex tasks, showcasing AI as a powerful productivity booster.

Identifying AI Opportunities: The Essential Checklist

Step 1: Assess Your Business Needs

Begin by conducting a comprehensive review of your business operations. Identify tasks that are repetitive or accuracy-dependent – prime candidates for AI enhancement. Crucially, engage in conversations with your team. They are entrenched in the daily workflow and can pinpoint inefficiencies with precision. Defining your business goals will also help tailor the AI solutions, ensuring they align with what you aim to accomplish post-integration.

Step 2: Research AI Applications

After honing in on your business needs, turn your attention to the vast field of AI applications. Seek out success stories, especially those resonating with your business type and size. Learn from peers who have reaped the benefits of AI, and keep abreast of emerging trends by attending industry-relevant events. Your goal here is to build a repository of knowledge that informs your AI selection process.

Step 3: Evaluate AI Solutions

With potential solutions on your radar, it's time to narrow the field. Organize demonstrations and in-depth discussions with AI vendors. Evaluate each solution against your unique business requirements, paying close attention to scalability, compatibility with existing systems, and budget constraints. It's a meticulous process but essential for informed decision-making.

Step 4: Pilot Test the AI Solution

Choose one or two AI solutions for a trial run within your operations. Set clear success metrics and apply the solution on a small scale. This pilot stage is invaluable, offering real-world insights into the AI's effectiveness and usability. Remember, feedback from your team is golden; they are the ones who will use this technology daily.

Step 5: Analyze Results and Make a Decision

Upon collecting pilot data, analyze the AI's impact. Did you notice a dip in operational costs? Has customer satisfaction spiked? Equally, take your team's experience into account. If the AI tool **proves** to be an ally in efficiency, you've cleared a significant hurdle toward full-scale implementation. Should results be mixed, consider optimizations or alternative solutions.

By following these structured steps, your journey toward AI integration becomes daunting and more of a strategic chess move. It is an opportunity to cast off the old ways and embrace a future where AI bolsters your business and becomes a beacon, guiding others to innovation and success.

Small businesses face unique challenges, from managing limited resources to staying competitive in an ever-evolving marketplace. AI integration is no longer a luxury reserved for large corporations; it is an essential tool for local businesses looking to cut costs and boost profits. This technological advancement offers a wealth of opportunities for small businesses to streamline operations, enhance customer experiences, and drive revenue growth. Despite initial investment concerns, the long-term benefits of AI greatly exceed the costs.

Case studies have consistently shown how small businesses that integrated AI solutions have experienced significant returns on investment. From predictive analytics improving inventory management to chatbots enhancing customer service, AI has proven instrumental in automating processes and identifying new business opportunities. For instance, a small retail store implemented AI-powered inventory management systems and saw a 30% decrease in overstocked items and a 20% increase in sales due to improved stock availability. Such tangible results demonstrate the transformative power of AI for local businesses.

One compelling example of AI enhancing small business operations is the story of 4th Generation Communication LLC. This innovative company developed an AI-powered chatbot that revolutionized customer engagement for countless small businesses. Using natural language processing and machine learning, the chatbot streamlined customer inquiries, provided personalized recommendations and even facilitated sales transactions. As a result, businesses that integrated the 4th Generation chatbot saw a substantial increase in customer satisfaction and retention, leading to accelerated revenue growth and strengthened market position.

AI integration is beneficial, sustainable, and **essential for local businesses aiming to cut costs and boost profits.** The competitive landscape demands efficiency and innovation, and AI arms small businesses with the tools to achieve both. By recognizing the indispensability of AI and embracing its potential, businesses can survive and thrive in today's dynamic market. The time to integrate AI is now, and its rewards are worth the investment.

Embrace the Potential

The potential of AI integration for local businesses is limitless. Learn how AI can transform operations and drive growth, positioning your business for success in the digital age.

The potential inefficiencies and lost sales from not adopting AI in today's competitive market can harm local businesses. These inefficiencies can manifest in various forms, from manual data entry errors to outdated forecasting methods, ultimately leading to a loss in productivity and increased operating costs. Without AI integration, businesses may struggle to keep up with competitors leveraging advanced technologies to streamline their operations and deliver exceptional customer experiences. The resulting decrease in competitiveness could lead to a loss of market share and missed revenue opportunities, further exacerbating the challenges faced by businesses that have yet to embrace AI.

The Pitfalls of Resistance

When businesses resist the integration of AI into their operations, they risk falling behind in an ever-evolving market. Failing to utilize AI-powered analytics and automation can lead to missed insights, inefficient processes, and a lack of agility in responding to changing consumer demands. This resistance can result in missed sales opportunities, reduced customer satisfaction, and decreased overall revenue.

Real-world Examples of AI Success

Consider the story of a local retail store that integrated AI-driven inventory management systems and customer analytics software. By leveraging these technologies, the store was able to optimize its inventory levels, track customer buying patterns, and implement targeted marketing campaigns, resulting in a significant increase in sales and customer satisfaction. Similarly, a local e-commerce business experienced substantial growth after implementing AI-powered chatbots to provide personalized customer support and recommendations, leading to a substantial increase in conversions and customer retention.

Case Studies in AI ROI

A prime example of AI delivering a tangible return on investment (ROI) can be seen in the case of a small manufacturing company that implemented AI-driven predictive maintenance. By leveraging AI to analyze equipment performance data and predict maintenance needs, the company was able to reduce downtime, extend the lifespan of machinery, and ultimately increase production capacity and revenue.

AI Chatbot Success Stories

One notable success story in AI chatbots comes from 4th Generation Communication LLC. Their AI chatbot solution has been instrumental in transforming the customer service operations of local businesses. By providing instant, personalized support to customers and streamlining the sales process, the chatbot has enabled businesses to enhance customer satisfaction and drive sales growth. A local restaurant, for example, saw a significant increase in online orders and table reservations after implementing the AI chatbot to handle customer inquiries and bookings, showcasing the clear impact of AI integration on business performance.

Understanding the potential inefficiencies, lost sales, and decreased competitiveness resulting from not adopting AI is crucial for local businesses aiming to thrive in today's market. By recognizing the real-world success stories of AI integration and the tangible ROI it delivers, businesses can gain valuable insights into the transformative power of AI and the competitive advantage it offers.

Integrating AI into your local business isn't just a step forward; it's a leap into efficiency that must be addressed. Consider the use case of a local retail store that incorporated an AI-powered inventory management system. This tool revolutionized its stock levels by predicting fluctuations in demand before they happened, ordering products just in time, **avoiding overstocking** and the resultant markdowns. This cut costs drastically and increased the store's profits by ensuring the freshest merchandise was available to customers, directly influencing their purchasing decisions. Tangible results like these underscore that **AI integration is a practical means to an enhanced bottom line** rather than just another tech trend.

AI doesn't only transform existing processes; it creates opportunities. Take, for example, a family-owned restaurant struggling with the disconnect between the kitchen's pace and customer orders during peak hours. By implementing an AI-driven analytical system, they could pinpoint bottlenecks in their service. The data showed that they could cut down table wait times by optimizing the order sequence and menu offerings, directly leading to serving more guests and boosting revenue. The result? **A happier clientele** and a significant uptick in evening sales.

Customer engagement and retention are pillars of a successful business. Knowing this, a local salon adopted a chatbot developed by 4th Generation Communication LLC. This intelligent chatbot offered personalized appointment scheduling and recommended services based on past visits. The AI's ability to remember individual preferences and suggest future appointments enhanced customer experience and saw an increase in repeat visits. This customization and attention to detail **fosters customer loyalty**—and with AI, this doesn't require extra staff or hours.

For many local businesses, marketing is often hit-or-miss. However, with AI's predictive analysis, a small boutique could focus its advertising spend on customers who were most likely to make a purchase, boosting its return on investment significantly. It harnessed AI to analyze traffic patterns and social media trends, targeting advertisements that were not just seen but acted upon. **The shift from blanket marketing to a targeted approach** meant that, although they were spending less, their marketing efforts were now more effective and lucrative.

Reducing operational costs is another frontier where AI has proven to be indispensable—a small manufacturing unit with limited resources integrated AI into its supply chain. By using machine learning to optimize delivery routes and inventory controls, the company reported a reduction in logistics costs by nearly 15%. Staff once bogged down by manual tracking could now focus on more strategic activities. It elevated the efficiency of their operations and reflected positively on their **financial health**.

Beyond cutting costs and boosting sales, AI delivers insights that are rich in potential. For instance, a local bookstore used AI algorithms to analyze purchase histories and browsing behaviors, allowing them to curate book recommendations that kept customers coming back. By understanding their customers better, they positioned themselves as a staple in the community, enhancing their **reputation as a business that knows and grows with its clientele**.

Investing in AI does not go unnoticed by customers. When patrons see a business employing modern technology to serve them better, it speaks volumes about the company's commitment to excellence. A local hardware store demonstrated this by introducing an AI-backed inventory query system. Customers could check stock in real-time via an app, saving time and frustration. This transparent and efficient approach attracted more business and even garnered **local media attention**—free marketing thanks to a decision to embrace AI.

To sum up, integrating AI into local business operations is not merely beneficial—it's a strategic imperative in the modern marketplace. The diverse applications of AI equip businesses with tools to trim excess costs, revitalize sales strategies, and deliver **unrivaled customer service**. As these case studies reveal, AI is the catalyst for transformation that can propel a local business into new realms of profit and efficiency. The advantage is not only in the technology itself but in the innovative mindset of those who dare to adopt it.

In today's competitive world, AI integration is beneficial and **essential** for local businesses aiming to cut costs and boost profits. The evidence is clear: businesses that embrace AI have the potential to not only survive but thrive in their respective markets. Take, for example, 4th Generation Communication LLC, a small telecommunication company that implemented an AI chatbot to improve customer service efficiency.**4th Generation Communication LLC** This move resulted in a 30% reduction in customer service costs and a 15% increase in customer satisfaction within just six months. This demonstrates the clear, tangible benefits that AI can bring to local businesses.

Understanding the potential inefficiencies, lost sales, and competitiveness of not adopting AI in today's market is crucial. Many businesses have fallen behind simply because they were unwilling or unable to adapt to the modern technological landscape. In contrast, companies like **Cloud9 Coffee Roasters** leveraged AI algorithms to optimize their supply chain, leading to a 20% reduction in inventory costs and a 10% increase in on-time deliveries. This success story serves as a testament to AI's strategic advantage, allowing businesses to survive and excel.

Exploring how AI can streamline operations, reduce costs, and drive revenue growth for local businesses is paramount. In the case of **Vibrant Dental Studio**, the implementation of AI-powered scheduling software led to a 40% reduction in administrative costs and a 25% increase in appointment bookings due to enhanced customer experience. This case study highlights the transformative potential of AI in simplifying processes, lowering expenses, and boosting revenue, thereby securing a competitive edge in the market.

By leveraging AI, businesses position themselves as leaders in their respective markets. The potential for an AI-driven transformation is no longer a mere possibility but a necessity. The evidence from case studies like those of **4th Generation Communication LLC**, **Cloud9 Coffee Roasters**, and **Vibrant Dental Studio** reveals the concrete benefits of integrating AI. By recognizing the essential nature of AI integration, local businesses can proactively drive their path toward increased profitability, streamlined operations, and sustained growth.

Chapter 5
Streamlining Customer Service with AI Chatbots

Through the plate glass window of the quaint corner café, the neon "Open" sign hummed softly in the half-light of an early dawn. Inside, Sam Ingram, a local small business owner, hunched over a wooden table cluttered with papers, his cup of coffee long cold as thoughts churned through his mind with the same relentless blend of hope and anxiety that colored the skyline. Sam's business was floundering – a ship struggling to stay afloat in the turbulent waters of rising customer service demands and the skyrocketing costs of employing enough staff to keep the bilge pumps going.

Across the way, the barista moved with balletic grace, her every motion an elegant and purposeful dance with steam and espresso. It offered a stark contrast to Sam's inner turmoil as he considered the leap into a technology that never tired – AI chatbots.

The persistent drone of city traffic outside was punctuated by the chirp of a lone sparrow seeking out the day's first meal, a reminder that life's progress was indifferent to individual predicaments. Sam had heard stories within his business network, tales of digital alchemy where ones and zeros coalesced into something nearly sentient – artificial constructs bearing the promise of infinite scalability. "Perhaps," Sam mused, the weight of empirical evidence leaning heavily on him, "this could be the pivot my business needs."

A text message buzzed on his phone: a case study from a fellow entrepreneur. 4th Generation Communication LLC's AI chatbot had not just stabilized their customer service. Still, it had turned it into a beacon of efficiency, drawing in weary travelers from the storm of unreliable support found elsewhere. The data spoke of reduced labor costs, and the numbers spun a tale of increased loyalty where customer satisfaction had blossomed into fervent advocacy.

Immersed in this digital reverie, Sam's gaze drifted to the young couple at the counter, laughing and sharing a croissant, a tangible rendition of the loyalty he sought to sow in his own clients – loyalty not born of shared moments but of relentless tireless service, an always-there-for-you digital companion.

A deep breath held the early morning chill from the air conditioning, a sensory prompt that delivered Sam back to the now. He knew that the investment in an AI companion like the chatbots of 4th Generation Communication LLC would not only be a cost-saving measure. It would be about sending out a beacon of innovation, a signal flare that would soar above the competition's conventional methods. It represented potential, like the sun peeking over the horizon – the start of something new, something brilliant.

Sam sipped his cold coffee – its bitterness a striking metaphor for the untapped potential before him. It was time to make a splash in an ocean of competitors, to navigate this new world of AI customer service where human fatigue never dimmed the light of availability and where a small business could stand giant-like, offering its patrons a titan's feast of responsiveness and care.

But would the warmth of human touch perish in the embrace of this digital dawn? Would loyalty be born of efficiency alone, or did the true essence of service still require something more human, something irreducibly organic?

Elevating Customer Engagement

With artificial intelligence revolutionizing how businesses operate, **AI chatbots** have emerged as a game-changer in customer service. By harnessing the power of these AI-driven assistants, local businesses can now offer round-the-clock support without the constraints of human limitations. This translates into *significant cost savings* by reducing the overhead of staffing, training, and managing a traditional customer service team. But the benefits don't end at financial reprieve; the ability to handle multiple concurrent interactions ensures customers are attended to promptly, fostering a high satisfaction rate pivotal for customer retention and word-of-mouth referrals.

AI chatbots empower businesses to meet the modern consumer's expectation of *instantaneous and efficient support*. SMEs that adopt this technology report decreased operational costs and an uptick in revenue stemming from improved customer experiences. Let's delve into the story of 4th Generation Communication LLC, a small business that transformed its customer engagement model using an AI chatbot. Within months, they experienced a surge in customer satisfaction and, as a result, enjoyed increased brand loyalty and a more robust bottom line.

Consider this: a customer has a pressing question at midnight. In the pre-AI era, they'd have to wait until business hours for a response. However, 4th Generation Communication LLC's AI chatbot can address inquiries 24/7, instantly providing the information or assistance needed. This responsiveness is more than a convenience—it's a critical component of customer satisfaction and loyalty in an age where delay can mean the loss of a sale or customer.

Furthermore, the *efficiency of AI chatbots* in handling concurrent inquiries cannot be overstated. One AI chatbot can manage what would take multiple human agents to accomplish, streamlining the customer service process and reducing queue times. This means customers receive the attention they deserve even during peak hours or promotional periods without costly staff expansions.

The ripple effects of such enhanced services are profound. Satisfied customers tend to share their experiences with others, which can lead to new customers without the added expense of traditional marketing campaigns. In turn, *customer trust and brand reputation* are strengthened, essential components of sustainable business growth.

In the next few paragraphs, we will discuss in depth how AI chatbots are the stalwarts of customer service for local businesses, aiding them to thrive financially while upholding exceptional 8-customer care. Emphasis will be placed on how businesses can implement this technology to achieve *increased profits, market dominance*, and a *high competitive edge* - all without overwhelming their teams or budgets.

By integrating chatbots into their operations, businesses are not only giving back to the community by providing better service. Still, they are also contributing to a more technologically advanced and efficient marketplace. We will explore the stories of several businesses that have successfully deployed AI chatbots, examining the tangible outcomes and the practices that paved the way for their successes. Prepare to unlock the transformative potential of AI for your local business.

In today's fast-paced business environment, customer service has become more significant. To stay competitive, businesses must be available to address customer inquiries and concerns 24/7. This is where AI chatbots offer cost-effective customer service without breaks. Unlike human representatives, AI chatbots don't require rest, enabling your business to provide round-the-clock customer support without incurring additional labor costs. Chatbots are always ready to engage with customers, ensuring no inquiry goes unanswered.

Furthermore, AI chatbots can handle multiple inquiries simultaneously. This means that, as a business owner, you can streamline your customer service operations while ensuring high levels of customer satisfaction. The ability to handle numerous queries at once increases efficiency, allowing your business to handle a larger volume of customer requests within a shorter period.

Moreover, AI chatbots can be programmed to understand and respond to inquiries in natural language, continuously learning from interactions to improve their responses over time. This means that customer inquiries can be resolved swiftly and accurately, further contributing to higher customer satisfaction. Customers appreciate prompt and accurate responses, resulting in increased loyalty and positive recommendations for your business.

Ultimately, leveraging AI chatbots for customer service can lead to substantial cost savings for your business while enhancing the overall customer experience. Implementing AI chatbots as part of your customer service strategy can significantly impact your bottom line, leading to increased operational efficiency and customer loyalty. With the ability to provide 24/7 support and handle multiple inquiries simultaneously, AI chatbots can revolutionize your customer service operations and drive greater success for your business.

Discover the potential of AI chatbots in streamlining your customer service operations and achieving substantial cost savings. Explore how chatbots efficiently manage multiple inquiries simultaneously, ensuring heightened customer satisfaction and driving revenue growth.

Understanding how chatbots can handle multiple inquiries simultaneously is crucial for small business owners looking to streamline their customer service operations. The ability of AI chatbots to efficiently manage numerous customer queries at once ensures high levels of customer satisfaction and significantly reduces the burden on human customer service representatives. The demand for instant responses and efficient problem resolution has remained the same in today's fast-paced business environment. AI chatbots, like those offered by 4th Generation Communication LLC, have proven invaluable tools in meeting these demands while driving cost savings and enhancing operational efficiency.

Case studies provide compelling evidence of how AI chatbots have helped small businesses achieve a positive return on investment. For instance, a local retail store implementing AI chatbot technology observed a 30% reduction in the average response time for customer inquiries while handling three times the volume of queries compared to human agents. This heightened customer satisfaction and enabled the retail store to reallocate human resources to other critical areas, contributing to a more holistic operational enhancement.

In another example, a boutique e-commerce business integrated 4th Generation Communication LLC's AI chatbot into its customer service framework and experienced a 40% increase in customer retention rates. The chatbot was pivotal in nurturing customer loyalty by efficiently addressing customer queries, providing personalized recommendations, and swiftly resolving issues. This translated into a tangible boost in repeat purchases and positive word-of-mouth referrals, ultimately contributing to revenue growth and sustainable business expansion.

4th Generation Communication LLC's AI chatbot allows businesses to enhance customer service capabilities and create a competitive edge. The chatbot's ability to manage multiple inquiries simultaneously and adapt and learn from interactions enables businesses to handle customer needs around the clock efficiently. These capabilities are rooted in advanced natural language processing and machine learning algorithms, empowering businesses to deliver personalized, context-aware responses that drive customer satisfaction and trust.

Leveraging 4th Generation Communication LLC's AI chatbot allows small businesses to ensure **24/7**

customer service without breaks while maintaining high service levels. This leads to direct cost savings associated with reduced labor expenditure and is a strategic investment in fostering long-term customer relationships. The efficiency and consistency offered by AI chatbots play a pivotal role in shaping positive customer experiences, laying the groundwork for sustained business growth and success.

In summary, the ability of AI chatbots to handle multiple inquiries simultaneously is a game-changer for small businesses seeking to streamline their customer service operations. Through real-world case studies and tangible success stories, it's evident that 4th Generation Communication LLC's AI chatbot has the potential to deliver measurable return on investment by driving cost savings, bolstering customer satisfaction, and catalyzing revenue growth. As businesses navigate the evolving landscape of customer service, embracing AI chatbots as a fundamental tool for operational enhancement and customer engagement is no longer an option but a strategic imperative.

The AI-Powered Customer Segmentation Model

When exploring the transformative effect of AI chatbots on customer loyalty and subsequent revenue growth, it's essential to conceptualize a structured approach that drives this impact. This is where the AI-Powered Customer Segmentation Model gains prominence. At its core, it encapsulates seven steps designed to analyze customer data through AI, culminating in strategic actions tailored to enhance customer experiences and foster loyalty. Let's delve into each component and understand how they collaboratively contribute to revenue growth by fostering increased customer loyalty and generating positive recommendations.

Data Collection

The bedrock of any consumer insight strategy is the collection of rich, detailed customer data. In the context of this model, data is sourced from various channels, including CRM systems, transaction records, and social media activities. For instance, a small local boutique leverages its online sales records and social media interactions to paint a detailed portrait of its clientele, guiding its marketing campaigns and product development. This foundational step is critical as it determines the granularity and effectiveness of the subsequent segmentation process.

Data Preparation

Once data is harvested, the preparatory refining process begins. **Data cleaning** and normalization ensure accuracy and uniformity, which is key to reliable AI analysis. Small businesses might underestimate this phase but consider a home improvement service that, through meticulous data preparation, discards irrelevant records, such as outdated customer contacts. By doing so, they focus their resources effectively on current customer needs and preferences, avoiding waste and enhancing the responsiveness of their service.

Feature Selection

Selecting the right features — the AI's variables to segment customers — is akin to choosing the correct lens to view a problem. This stage uses techniques like correlation analysis to prioritize the data that best distinguishes customer types. A specialty coffee shop, for instance, might discover that purchase frequency and average transaction value are key indicators of customer loyalty and thus segment their customers accordingly.

AI Model Training

In this phase, the chosen data is fed into a clustering algorithm, training it to identify natural groupings within the customer base. Small businesses benefit immensely here, as even a modest local florist can use such algorithms to distinguish between casual buyers and event planners, allowing for targeted marketing and personalized service.

Cluster Analysis

After the model is trained, the resulting clusters are scrutinized to extract valuable insights into each customer segment. Visualizations such as heatmaps can reveal, for example, a cluster of customers in a pet store that prefers organic pet food, prompting the store to stock more of that product line and tailor their communication to meet this specific demand.

Segment Profiling

Profiling is where the narrative of each customer segment comes to life. Here, businesses synthesize behavioral patterns and demographic characteristics to understand the essence of each cluster. By recognizing a segment of avid young adult genre readers, a local bookstore can launch a book club to deepen their engagement and turn them into brand advocates.

Targeted Strategy Development

The final step translates insights into action. Personalized strategies are developed for each segment, optimizing marketing efforts and product offerings and ensuring resources are balanced on one-size-fits-all solutions. For instance, a home tech provider could identify a segment interested in smart home automation and create tailored resources educating them on the benefits, simplifying choices, and encouraging upgrades.

By embracing the AI-Powered Customer Segmentation Model, small businesses gain a robust framework to enhance their customer service approach via AI chatbots. Providing personalized experiences based on detailed customer profiling leads to higher satisfaction, often shared through recommendations, incrementally contributing to revenue growth. While ensuring customer needs are anticipated and met, businesses foster loyalty, proving that AI investments pay dividends beyond immediate cost savings. As customer data evolves, so does this model, maintaining its relevance and effectiveness in an ever-changing market landscape.

In the fast-paced realm of customer service, AI chatbots present a transformative solution for local businesses. Round-the-clock support can boost customer loyalty and recommendations, ultimately driving revenue growth. Meeting the expectations of an always-on customer base and delivering cost-effective assistance are crucial. This ensures customer satisfaction and reduces the expenses of employing customer service agents 24/7.

Furthermore, the ability of chatbots to handle multiple inquiries simultaneously presents a significant advantage. By promptly and effectively addressing the needs of numerous customers simultaneously, these advanced systems ensure that customer satisfaction remains consistently high, enhancing your business's reputation as reliable and customer-focused. This capability alone can cultivate greater customer loyalty and referrals, thus profoundly impacting your business's revenue growth.

Let's illustrate these insights with a real case study. 4th Generation Communication LLC, a small telecom company, enhanced its customer service operations by implementing an AI chatbot. This move enabled them to offer round-the-clock support, significantly reducing the need for additional customer service staff. Consequently, the ROI from implementing the chatbot had a profoundly positive impact on their profitability.

In another instance, a local online retailer integrated an AI chatbot to handle customer inquiries. As a result of the chatbot's ability to address **multiple inquiries simultaneously**, the retailer saw a stark improvement in **customer satisfaction** and a notable increase in **revenue**, highlighting the undeniable influence of AI chatbots on business success.

The next time you ponder how to streamline your customer service operations, consider the profound impact AI chatbots can have on your business. Their ability to provide **24/7 cost-effective support**, handle **multiple inquiries simultaneously**, and indirectly contribute to revenue growth through increased loyalty and recommendations is nothing short of transformational.

Chapter 6
Leveraging Chatbot Data for Business Insights

In the bustling heart of a small town's retail hub, with streets lined with family-owned businesses, Sophie's boutique exuded a quaint charm. The chime of the bell above the door marked the entrance of every customer, a melodic soundtrack to everyday commerce. Inside, racks of clothing whispered of cotton and silk, and the air carried the subtle scent of cedar from the polished floor beneath a parade of patrons.

The store's owner, Sophie, stood behind the register, her mind a bristling hive of scattered thoughts, excitement edged with concern. She mulled over her recent decision to integrate an AI chatbot system into her business—the avant-garde spirit of 4th Generation Communication LLC's technology. She recalled the stories of other shopkeepers, tales of transformation where chatbots opened doorways to customer hearts and needs.

Outside, the afternoon sun painted the sky with a mellow amber as shoppers navigated the trodden paths of Sophie's store, their conversations a tapestry of needs and wishes. As the murmur of patrons floated through the air, Sophie envisioned the silhouettes of data points and customer patterns that her new digital ally could unveil. It was a stark contrast—this gallery of invisible insights against the palpable warm woolen dresses just a finger's touch away.

The neighboring bookstore owner, Julian, stepping in to peruse Sophie's latest collection and share his experience, became the unexpected catalyst. His bookstore, once quiet and still as stagnant water, now brimmed with life, thanks to his chatbot's precise recommendations. Julian spoke serenely, his narratives weaving through the bookstore's revitalized sales, a stark outcome rooted in numeric analysis yet reflected in every human interaction.

As the day waned and the last customer's laughter faded away, Sophie locked the door. Above, the stars blinked into existence, mirroring the potential of the data points yet to be collected by her chatbot. The fusion of analytics and empathy promised a bright future with prospective profits and poignant connections. With its unerring algorithms, would the chatbot bridge the gap between her aspirations and the concrete reality of business growth? In the depth of night, could her little boutique become a beacon of tailored experiences in this ever-shifting tapestry of market desires?

Could a string of code lead her to the elusive rhythm of customers' hearts, synching her offerings with the unspoken narratives of those who walked through her door?

Unleashing the Power of Conversation: Transform Your Data Into Dollars

Chatbots have evolved beyond basic customer service tools; they now serve as potent data capture devices, unlocking unparalleled business insights. By leveraging these insights, businesses can fine-tune their operations and marketing strategies to align precisely with customer behaviors and preferences. Local businesses that leverage these insights can tailor their strategies to meet their audience's needs effectively, transforming interactions into strategic advantages.

The magic of chatbots lies in their meticulous data analysis. They are robust sources of **qualitative** and **quantitative** data, providing a dual-lens into the consumer's world. They can track common inquiries, gauge sentiment, and identify market trends, offering a **360-degree view** of your customer base. This dynamic flow of information is critical for local businesses aiming to make **informed decisions** swiftly and confidently.

Deploying these digital assistants strategically in local businesses can drive significant profit growth and optimize resource allocation. Chatbot insights can better align with customer needs by informing product development and refining marketing campaigns, leading to market dominance.

This chapter will guide you through recognizing the data potential of chatbots, understanding the depth of insights they can provide, and exploring the **benefits** of leveraging this data. **Position your local business at the forefront** of innovation and customer satisfaction by tapping into the insights offered by chatbots, shaping your strategies around **real-time** customer data.

AI Solutions: Blueprint to Business Brilliance

Here is a step-by-step process to roll out AI solutions, including chatbots, for collecting and utilizing customer data to **boost** your local business.

Step 1: Plan and Prepare

Draft a **comprehensive implementation plan** outlining your goals, timeline, and resources. Assess your technological readiness and **allocate** a **dedicated team** or project manager to spearhead the rollout. This phase sets the **foundation** for a successful AI integration, eliminating guesswork and aligning your team with a common vision.

Step 2: Data Preparation

Pinpoint and **prepare the necessary data**. Clean and organize it to uphold **data integrity**. Data sources must be integrated with your new AI tools, preparing your business for **real-time** analytics and insights.

Step 3: Training and Integration

Educate your team on how to **harness** the AI tools effectively. Collaborate with AI providers for **seamless** tech integration and rigorously **test** to ensure it fits your business needs like a glove.

Step 4: Monitor and Optimize

Implement monitoring systems to track your AI tool's **performance**. Continuously **analyze** data to refine and **optimize** your AI's performance. Maintain a **feedback channel** with your team to enhance the tool's usability iteratively.

Step 5: Scaling and Expanding

Upon mastering AI in one area, **scale** your triumph across other departments. Scout for **additional AI opportunities** throughout your operations to **maximize** benefits, and regularly update your knowledge on the **latest AI advancements** to stay ahead of the curve.

From Insights to Acumen: Real-World Success with AI

Case studies and real-world applications underscore the potential ROI of implementing AI. For instance, a local boutique leveraging a **chatbot tailored by 4th Generation Communication LLC** saw a marked **increase in online sales** and improved customer satisfaction scores. By analyzing chat data, they fine-tuned their inventory to match customer preferences, leading to more targeted marketing campaigns and a better shopping experience.

Another case involves a family-owned restaurant implementing a chatbot to handle reservations and answer FAQs. The AI-driven analytics provided insights into peak hours, customer menu preferences, and common questions. This led to a more streamlined service, targeted menu changes, and a **higher turnover rate** during busy hours.

Remember, aligning operations with customer data is not the final destination—it marks a path of constant enhancement. By diligently adhering to these principles, local businesses can harness AI and chatbot data to excel, take the lead, and drive innovation in their respective industries.

Chatbots are not just tools for customer service; they are also powerful data collection and analysis tools. The data collected by chatbots during customer interactions provides valuable insights into customer preferences and behavior. Every interaction with a chatbot yields a goldmine of information that can inform product development, marketing strategies, and overall business decisions.

By examining the data collected from chatbot interactions, businesses can uncover patterns in customer behavior, preferences, and pain points. For example, if a chatbot consistently receives inquiries about a specific product feature, it signals a potential area for improvement or further promotion. Similarly, if customers frequently ask for assistance with a particular process, it could indicate a need for simplification or better user guidance.

Leveraging chatbot data enables businesses to gain deeper insights into their customer's needs and preferences, establishing a robust basis for strategic decision-making. By aligning their operations with customer demands and market trends, businesses can streamline resource utilization, craft precise marketing strategies, and create products and services that truly connect with their customer base.

In one case study, a small business in the hospitality industry used chatbot data to identify the most frequently asked questions by potential guests. By analyzing this data, the business was able to update its website and booking system to provide clearer information, resulting in a significant increase in direct bookings and a reduction in customer support inquiries.

Another example is a small e-commerce business that utilized chatbot data to identify customer preferences and purchasing behavior trends. This insight allowed the business to tailor their marketing campaigns and recommend products more effectively, resulting in a notable increase in conversion rates and customer satisfaction.

The data gathered by chatbots goes beyond mere interactions; it holds a wealth of valuable insights that can fuel business expansion and triumph. When utilized strategically, this data becomes a compass for businesses, aiding them in strategic decision-making, streamlining operations, and ultimately boosting their bottom line.

The next section will explore how chatbot data can transform product development, marketing strategies, and overall business decisions.

Utilizing chatbot data is an invaluable resource for businesses looking to inform product development, marketing strategies, and overall business decisions. By leveraging the insights collected through chatbot interactions, businesses can gain a deep understanding of customer preferences and behaviors, which can drive informed decision-making and strategic planning. The actionable insights from chatbot data can be transformative, leading to improved products, targeted marketing, and optimized operations that align closely with customer needs and market trends.

Product Development:

Chatbot data can provide crucial insights into customer preferences, pain points, and frequently asked questions. By analyzing this data, businesses can gain a clear understanding of customer needs and desires, allowing for the development of products and services tailored to meet those specific demands. For example, 4th Generation Communication LLC's AI chatbot helped a small business in the fashion industry by identifying common customer queries related to sizing, colors, and return policies. This data was then utilized to develop a new range of products that addressed these concerns, leading to increased customer satisfaction and sales.

Marketing Strategies:

Understanding customer behavior patterns and preferences through chatbot data can significantly impact marketing strategies. By identifying which products or services generate the most interest or receive the highest volume of inquiries, businesses can tailor their marketing efforts to focus on these key offerings. Additionally, chatbot data can uncover valuable demographic information, allowing for targeted marketing campaigns that resonate with specific customer segments. For instance, a small health and wellness business utilized chatbot data to identify its customer base's most common health concerns. This information was then utilized to create personalized marketing messages that directly addressed these pain points, significantly increasing engagement and sales.

Overall Business Decisions:

Chatbots' data offers valuable insights for strategic business decisions. Whether optimizing inventory or enhancing customer service, these insights drive operational choices. By analyzing customer queries, businesses can spot trends that signal the need for operational changes. For instance, a small e-commerce store leveraged chatbot data to identify increased demands for expedited shipping. Consequently, the store revised its shipping policies to provide quicker delivery, meet evolving customer needs, and gain a competitive advantage.

The stories of small businesses utilizing 4th Generation Communication LLC's AI chatbot are just a few examples of how leveraging chatbot data can lead to tangible, positive outcomes. These real-world case studies highlight how businesses can achieve a strong return on investment by incorporating chatbot data into their product development, marketing strategies, and overall business decisions. By using an AI chatbot, businesses access a wealth of actionable insights that can drive meaningful improvements across various facets of their operations.

The Power of Precision: Chatbot Data as a Compass

Chatbots have introduced a new era of precision in understanding and responding to customer needs. Take, for instance, the transformation 4th Generation Communication LLC experienced after integrating an AI chatbot into their customer service operations. By analyzing customer inquiries and request patterns, the chatbot provided insights that led to refining its communication strategy. As a result, the company achieved a **25% reduction in service resolution time** and an uptick in customer satisfaction ratings, underscoring the chatbot's efficacy in delivering actionable business intelligence.

Elevating Customer Experience with Data-Driven Insights

Aligning operations with customer expectations is a critical aspect of contemporary business strategy, and chatbot data analysis is at the heart of this alignment. Businesses can identify areas where customers seek more information or face challenges by tracking the frequency of specific queries or concerns. For example, a surge in questions about a particular product feature might indicate a need for clearer documentation or additional staff training. This proactive approach to customer issues **enhances the user experience** and cultivates a reputation for attentive service.

Streamlining with Segmentation: Chatbot Analytics and Marketing

Chatbot interactions aren't just conversations but a goldmine of segmentation data. Businesses can precisely tailor marketing campaigns by categorizing customers based on their inquiries and behavior. A local boutique, through chatbot analytics, identified that a significant portion of their clientele was interested in eco-friendly products. This insight led to a targeted marketing campaign that resulted in a **40% increase in sales of sustainable items**, illustrating the direct impact of data-informed marketing decisions.

Anticipating Market Trends with Granular Customer Data

Anticipation is the name of the game in a fast-paced market. Chatbots provide predictive analytics by capturing customer moods and preference shifts. For instance, if chatbot data highlights a growing interest in virtual consultations across several industries, businesses can leverage this information to *pivot their service offerings*, staying ahead of emerging trends. This strategic foresight enables companies to invest resources in developing offerings more likely to resonate with their customer base, potentially increasing market share.

Innovating with Confidence: Product Development Fueled by Customer Insights

Product innovation can be risky, especially for small businesses. However, chatbots can significantly de-risk this process by providing insights into what customers seek. An artisanal coffee shop used its chatbot data to detect customers' interest in cold brew. This led to introduction of a new cold brew line, which quickly became a bestseller. By **leveraging chatbot insights for product development**, the coffee shop could innovate confidently, knowing they were responding to genuine customer demand.

Resource Optimization: Chatbot Data as a Guide

Beyond customer insights, chatbot data can greatly enhance operational efficiency. By analyzing chatbot interactions, businesses can optimize their resource allocation. A small tech startup used chatbot data to realize that most of its customer support requests occurred during the late afternoon. By adjusting staff schedules to meet this demand, they **reduced wait times and increased customer satisfaction**, showcasing the operational benefits of chatbot data analysis.

Making Informed Decisions with a Data-Driven Approach

Chatbot analytics empower small businesses to make well-informed decisions in today's data-centric environment. A local bookstore, for instance, harnessed chatbot data, revealing a high demand for book recommendations in specific genres. Responding to this insight, they initiated a curated recommendation program. This move not only thrilled customers but also boosted sales in those genres by a remarkable 30%. They could make strategic decisions that led to a successful initiative by carefully analyzing chatbot interactions.

Cultivating Loyalty Through Personalized Interactions

Lastly, the capacity of chatbots to create personalized experiences cannot be understated. IVR (Interactive Voice Response) systems transformed when a small insurance firm upgraded to a chatbot system capable of recalling customer history and preferences. This shift led to a **notable increase in customer retention**, as clients felt acknowledged and valued. Personalization, informed by chatbot data, became a cornerstone of their customer relationship strategy.

The practical applications of chatbot data are vast and varied, demonstrating that businesses survive and thrive when operations are in tune with customer needs and market trends. In harnessing this AI-driven intel, small businesses can make strategic leaps, ensuring they are not just responding to the current market but actively shaping their future within it.

Incorporating AI chatbots into business operations can yield essential insights and drive informed decision-making. Businesses can gain a competitive edge by recognizing how chatbots collect and analyze data to uncover customer preferences and behavior. Through a deep understanding of how chatbot data informs product development, marketing strategies, and overall business decisions, companies can align their operations with customer needs and market trends, setting the stage for unprecedented success.

Utilize Chatbot Data for Holistic Business Improvement

AI-driven chatbot data is a powerful tool for deeply understanding customers' behaviors, preferences, and pain points. Leveraging this data enables your business to refine its product development, enhance marketing strategies, and make informed decisions across the organization. This approach allows for a more efficient allocation of resources, leading to increased profits and a sustainable competitive advantage.

Realize Tangible ROI Through AI-Driven Insights

Consider the case of a local restaurant implementing AI chatbots to handle customer inquiries and gather feedback. The restaurant discovered key patterns in customer preferences and sentiments toward their menu items by analyzing the data collected from these interactions. Armed with this invaluable insight, the restaurant optimized its menu offerings and tailored its marketing strategies, resulting in a significant increase in customer satisfaction and a boost in revenue.

4th Generation Communication LLC's AI Chatbot - A Path to Success

Picture a local boutique leveraging the AI-powered chatbot solution 4th Generation Communication LLC developed. This dynamic chatbot streamlined customer interactions and provided detailed insights into buying patterns and product preferences. By harnessing this information, the boutique identified trending fashion styles and adjusted its inventory accordingly, leading to a notable increase in sales and customer loyalty.

The potential for AI chatbots to revolutionize small businesses is undeniable. By harnessing the power of chatbot data, businesses can uncover pivotal insights, optimize their operations, and achieve remarkable returns on investment. As you navigate the upcoming chapters, remember the transformative impact AI-driven technologies can have on your business, propelling you toward sustained growth and prosperity.

Chapter 7
Demystifying AI: A Practical Business Tool

In the stillness of a small town's early hours, before the dawn's first light whispered through the window panes, Miriam set to work in the backroom that housed the heart of her floral shop. Fragrant blooms crowded the counters, a chaotic harmony of colors destined for carefully curated arrangements. Today, the quiet was different. It was a silence filled with contemplation, a backdrop for the turning gears of change.

Miriam cradled a pale rosebud between skillful fingers, thoughts of the day ahead unfurled like the petals themselves. Though small in scale, her cherished business thrived on connections as delicate and vital as the stamens she tended. She considered the recent conversation that had watered the seed of innovation in her mind—a fellow store owner's success with a simple yet effective AI—a chatbot named "GreetWell," crafted by 4th Generation Communication LLC.

It addressed customers by name, remembered their favorite blossoms, and even offered care tips for their purchases. Her peer's glowing account spoke not just of increased sales but of time reclaimed—time that could be spent crafting beauty rather than answering the ceaseless call of queries and phone orders.

Miriam placed the finished rose arrangement onto the countertop, its scent a sweet punctuation in the room. She pondered over the narrative of 4th Generation Communication's AI and how GreetWell could provide the bloom of efficiency and personalized service she longed for. Debating the practicality, her mind circled back to the hard facts, the case studies. The boutique had seen a 30% reduction in time spent on customer inquiries after GreetWell took on the mundane task of answering frequent questions.

Her heart swelled with the hope of what her shop might become with those hours reclaimed—the community events she could sponsor, the local artists she could feature, the new designs she could dream up.

As dawn finally broke, glowing on the modest storefront, Miriam brushed a loose strand from her cheek. She imagined the shop door swinging open, customers coming with smiles and leaving with GreetWell's digital footprint guiding their experience, enhancing the personal touch that her store was known for.

A regular, Mrs. DeWitt, came in, a kindly woman whose appreciation for lilies was well-known. Miriam greeted her with her customary warmth, while GreetWell would have already known to prepare a bouquet of the freshest Asiatic lilies, something Miriam admired.

Leaving Mrs. DeWitt to peruse today's assortment, Miriam returned to the workbench to her canvas of petals and leaves. A stray ray of sunlight caught on a vase, sending prisms dancing across the walls, a silent promise of potential waiting to be grasped.

AI might be a tool of the technological age, but to Miriam, it was more—the texture of a petal-soft innovation, a scent of progress amidst the familiar fragrance. Could this be the pulse of tomorrow for local businesses like hers? Could a GreetWell introduce the next chapter in her story? And, what might that chapter hold when the simplicity of a conversation takes on the artful intelligence of the future?

From Fiction to Function: The Real-World AI You Can't Afford to Overlook

Artificial Intelligence (AI) has rapidly transitioned from a buzzword reserved for Silicon Valley think tanks and sci-fi films to an indispensable tool for enterprises large and small. Its potential for local businesses is profound yet often obscured by misconceptions of complexity and scale. Today, with technological advancements, AI is not just for corporations with deep pockets but is an accessible solution for cost savings and efficiency improvements for small businesses. Understanding and implementing AI-like chatbots can be the difference between thriving and merely surviving in the current business landscape. This chapter aims to bridge the gap between AI myth and practical business reality, offering the building blocks necessary for leveraging AI's full potential.

Small, smart steps can lead to significant leaps in operational efficiency. Contrary to popular belief, introducing AI into your business process can be done without overhauling your entire system. Starting with a single function, such as customer service, can yield measurable improvements. Take the case of a local bakery that implemented a simple chatbot on its website. Orders that once took minutes to process manually were handled instantaneously, allowing staff to focus on baking rather than administrative tasks. Consequently, operating costs plummeted, and customer satisfaction soared. It's a prime example of low-barrier AI technologies creating high-impact results.

In demolishing the myth that AI is too sophisticated for the average business, it is crucial to recognize the **practical benefits it offers local enterprises**. From optimizing inventory management to personalizing customer interactions, AI tools can streamline operations in a way that previously required expensive expert consultants and time-consuming manual analyses. For instance, a family-owned hardware store utilized AI to forecast demand trends, resulting in a 15% reduction in overstock and a much healthier cash flow.

The advancements in accessible AI provide tangible benefits that move it directly from the fringes of business technology to the core of everyday operations. Concrete examples abound of AI's role in bolstering **business improvement**. A flower shop might employ a chatbot to handle common customer queries, saving time for more creative aspects of the business, like arrangement design or marketing strategies. With the automated assistance handling regular tasks, the shop can operate more fluidly and with better allocation of human resources.

It's imperative for small business owners to understand that AI doesn't replace human interaction but enhances it. By excavating the data businesses collect, AI helps make informed decisions. Imagine a local car repair shop implementing an AI system to track part replacements. Not only did it streamline inventory, but it also offered insights into supplier performance, leading to better negotiations and improved margins.

AI's role as a community improver should be noticed too. When businesses operate more efficiently, they can offer better service, contribute to local employment, and have a greater impact on their community. When a small clinic adopts AI to manage patient records and appointments, it doesn't just serve the clinic's interests. Still, it considerably improves patient experiences, demonstrating a commitment to service excellence that resonates community-wide.

To conclude, this chapter serves as a practical guide, stripping away the mystique of Artificial Intelligence and presenting it as an accessible, potent tool for enhancing local business operations. Through instructive insights, case studies, and a focus on actionable advice, we will reveal how AI is not a looming giant but rather a powerful ally to help your business scale new heights.

Artificial Intelligence is not just for tech giants; it's a practical tool that can provide tangible benefits for local businesses, demystifying the misconception that AI is out of reach for small enterprises. Even small businesses can experience cost savings and efficiency gains by leveraging accessible AI technologies like chatbots. These innovative AI applications can streamline customer interactions, improve operational efficiency, and drive business growth.

The chatbot facilitated seamless customer interactions, and AI-enabled significantly reduced the number of support staff needed to handle queries, leading to a marked decrease in operational costs. **The chatbot facilitated seamless customer interactions, and AI-enabled significantly reduced the number of support staff needed to handle queries, leading to a marked decrease in operational costs.** This efficient use of AI-enabled the business to reallocate resources to other critical areas and further enhance the customer experience, resulting in increased customer satisfaction and higher sales.

The chatbot's ability to engage with potential customers 24/7 improved customer responsiveness and it led to a substantial increase in the number of leads generated. **The chatbot's ability to engage with potential customers 24/7 improved customer responsiveness and it led to a substantial increase in the number of leads generated.** As a result, the agency witnessed a significant boost in sales and conversions, all while minimizing the need for additional human resources to handle customer queries.

4th Generation Communication LLC's AI chatbot is a powerful example of how integrating AI into a small business can lead to measurable ROI. By enabling seamless customer interactions, personalized assistance, and instant responses, the chatbot effectively enhances the overall customer experience while reducing operational costs. Through this technology, small businesses can achieve a competitive edge by offering personalized, efficient, round-the-clock customer support, ultimately driving sales and revenue growth.

By understanding how AI technologies like chatbots have delivered tangible benefits for small businesses, you can envision the potential impact on your own enterprise. Let's explore the practical benefits of AI for local businesses and debunk the myth that AI is only for tech giants.

AI is not just for tech giants. It can provide practical benefits for local businesses, enhancing efficiency, cutting costs, and improving customer interactions. By leveraging accessible AI technologies like chatbots, even small enterprises can experience significant returns, demystifying the misconception that AI is out of reach. AI can level the playing field and empower local businesses to compete with larger corporations, making it a valuable tool for growth and success.

One compelling case study is the story of a small e-commerce store that integrated an AI-powered chatbot into its website. This chatbot efficiently handled customer inquiries, provided personalized recommendations, and even processed orders. The result? Not only did the store see a significant reduction in customer service costs, but it also experienced an increase in sales due to the personalized assistance offered by the chatbot. This small business saw a positive ROI from implementing AI, demonstrating that practical benefits are within reach, regardless of business size.

Another example comes from a local restaurant that adopted an AI-driven reservation system. By leveraging AI to manage table bookings and optimize seating arrangements, the restaurant significantly increased its efficiency during peak hours, improving customer satisfaction and higher table turnover. The AI-driven system also helped identify customer preferences, allowing the restaurant to offer personalized experiences and upsell promotions, boosting revenue. This practical application of AI directly impacted the business's bottom line, showcasing the tangible benefits accessible to local businesses.

Now, look closer at **4th Generation Communication LLC**'s AI chatbot, which was designed specifically for small businesses. Imagine a local hardware store implementing this chatbot on its website. Customers visiting the site can interact with the chatbot to inquire about product availability, receive recommendations based on their needs, and even place orders directly through the chat interface. The hardware store reduces the load on its customer service staff and provides a seamless and personalized experience to its online customers, leading to higher customer satisfaction and increased sales.

The AI chatbot can also be integrated into the store's social media platforms, allowing customers to engage in real-time conversations and receive immediate assistance for their queries. This enhances the store's online presence and builds trust and loyalty among its customer base. As a result, the hardware store experiences improved customer retention and increased repeat business, directly impacting its revenue and long-term sustainability.

We can understand that AI is not just reserved for tech giants by demystifying AI's practical benefits to local businesses. Small enterprises can leverage AI technologies like chatbots to streamline operations, improve customer experiences, and drive growth. The examples of the e-commerce store, restaurant, and hardware store showcase how AI can deliver tangible returns for small businesses, dispelling the myth that AI is out of reach for them. It's time for local businesses to recognize the practical advantages of AI and harness its power to soar ahead in their respective markets.

AI-Driven Decision-Making Model

Introducing AI into a business's decision-making process can revolutionize its operations, particularly following a structured model. This model is a blueprint for intelligently and methodically incorporating AI into daily business practices. By adhering to the AI-driven Decision-Making Model, companies of all sizes can harness AI to make more data-driven, insightful decisions that lead to tangible improvements in performance and efficiency.

Define Decision-Making Goals

The first step in the AI-driven Decision-Making Model is to set clear, measurable goals. **Decision-making goals** vary from optimizing pricing strategies to enhancing inventory management. For example, a local grocery store may use AI to decide on stock levels for perishable goods to reduce waste and increase profitability.

Identify Relevant Data

After defining goals, the next task is identifying relevant data that informs those goals. Data is the lifeblood of AI; it becomes valuable when it's comprehensive, accurate, and reflective of the business's environment. The grocery store would gather data from sales records, supplier schedules, and weather forecasts, knowing that these factors can all influence buying patterns.

Data Analysis and Insights

The raw data now needs to be transformed into actionable insights. Here, AI shines by employing classification algorithms, regression analysis, and more techniques to deduce patterns and trends. Let's illustrate with a case study: a local clothing retailer employs machine learning models to identify styles and sizes most likely to sell during different seasons, enabling better stock management and targeted promotions.

Decision Optimization

With insights in hand, businesses must determine the optimal decisions. AI can help by using **optimization techniques** to propose the best courses of action. For the clothing retailer, this could mean an AI system recommending the ideal quantity of each clothing item to order, thus maximizing sales while minimizing surplus inventory.

Decision Validation

Before implementing any decision recommended by AI, validation is essential. Techniques such as A/B testing or scenario analysis can anticipate outcomes and evaluate decision impact. For instance, if the AI suggests a new pricing strategy, the retailer may test it with a small market segment to assess customer response and sales performance.

Decision Execution and Monitoring

Once a decision passes validation, it's time for execution and ongoing monitoring. AI can also aid here by tracking KPIs and adjusting real-time strategies based on actual performance data. This continuous loop ensures the business stays agile and responsive to market dynamics.

The final component emphasizes learning and improvement. Every decision, successful or not, is a learning opportunity. Feedback loops and post-analysis are key, helping to refine future AI applications. This reflects a commitment to ongoing enhancement, mirroring the ethos of community service by fostering improvement that benefits the business and its customers and area.

By following this cohesive framework, local businesses can gradually demystify the complexity of AI and start enjoying the practical benefits it offers. The AI-driven Decision-Making Model is more than a theoretical concept. It's a dynamic tool that evolves with your business, helping you navigate the myriad of choices daily while driving towards more substantial growth and efficiency.

In summary, AI is not just a tool for tech giants; it's a practical business tool that can drive cost savings, efficiency gains, and overall improvement for local enterprises. By incorporating accessible technologies like chatbots, small businesses can begin to unlock the benefits of AI without the need for significant investment or technical expertise.

4th Generation Communication LLC's AI chatbot is a prime example of how AI can revolutionize local businesses. Take the case of a small cafe struggling to keep up with customer inquiries and reservations. By implementing 4th Generation Communication LLC's AI chatbot, the cafe could handle customer queries, manage reservations, and recommend personalized menu items based on customer preferences. As a result, the cafe saw increased customer satisfaction, higher table turnover, and a significant revenue boost.

Similarly, another local business, a boutique clothing store, integrated the AI chatbot to enhance the shopping experience for its customers. The chatbot helped customers find the perfect outfit, provided fashion tips, and offered personalized recommendations based on previous purchases. This led to increased customer loyalty, higher average sales per customer, and a notable reduction in the time spent on repetitive inquiries, allowing the staff to focus on more critical tasks.

The practical benefits of AI for local businesses are clear. By embracing accessible technologies like chatbots, businesses can streamline operations, personalize customer experiences, and drive growth. *The demystification of AI paves the way for businesses to leverage this powerful tool for tangible, real-world benefits.*

As you consider how AI can fit into your business strategy, consider the specific pain points you want to address and the outcomes you hope to achieve. Then, explore how 4th Generation Communication LLC's AI chatbot can be tailored to meet your unique business needs, whether streamlining customer service, optimizing sales processes, or personalizing the customer experience.

Remember, AI is not just a futuristic concept; it's a practical, accessible, and impactful tool that can drive your business forward. It's time to harness its potential for your business's success.

Chapter 8
Accessible AI Solutions for Local Businesses

The sun hung low in the expanse, a flaming medallion drowning in the vast horizon. Elena's curiosity shop was set against the dusky sky, a nook of wonder amidst the sleepy town that prided itself on small, hearty businesses. The little bell over the storefront tinkled as the door creaked open, a daily ritual as reliable as the sunrise. But today, Elena stood behind the counter, ruminating over the crux of her business's existential dilemma.

The month had ushered in a whisper of change, or was it a clamor? A local eatery had just doubled its customer base, seemingly overnight, with the charm of clever banter and timely service, not by human hands, but by binary code—a chatbot, they called it, a herald of AI for the average Joe.

The thought serpentined around Elena's mind as she unpacked a box of antiquities, each item holding a tale as long as its history. The shop was her heart's labor, a mosaic of the old and the mysterious, yet her ledger told stories of numbers that refused to romanticize. Perhaps, she mused, the integration of such a digital assistant could steer a tide of fortune her way, beckoning to the young, the tech-savvy, the seekers of efficiency in conversation.

She recalled a florist two blocks down who had shared the seeds of his success over coffee—predictive analytics. He no longer rued losses over unsold bouquets or scrambled in the wake of a sudden demand. His knowledge was now seasoned by algorithms predicting the ebb and flow of his floral inventory. Could such a calculated foresight be the companion to her intuition?

The flicker of her laptop screen in the corner beckoned, a gateway to boundless opportunities. With a decisive breath, Elena resolved to marry the wisdom of the past with the promise of the future—a foray into accessible AI solutions for a shop steeped in time-worn tales.

She engaged with tales of 4th Generation Communication LLC, where digital minds had reshaped fates with AI-driven charm. As she read case studies, each a testament to the transformative power of technology for the smallest enterprises, Elena felt a burgeoning sense of kinship with these pioneers who dared to evolve.

The clock on the wall chimed the hour, mixing with the hum of her thoughts. A new era of business beckoned subtle yet assertive, much like the inevitable march of time just beyond her window. Within this moment of soft twilight and contemplative silence, perhaps one might wonder if small businesses could indeed wield the might of AI, not as a daunting titan, but as a tailored ally in their quest for continuity and growth.

In a world that relished the grandiose, could the modest dreams of a local shopkeeper find solace and success within the folds of artificial intelligence?

Demystifying AI for Your Storefront: From Myth to Money Maker

Small and medium-sized businesses are the backbone of local economies, and in today's competitive marketplace, standing out requires tenacity and innovation. The age of artificial intelligence (AI) has ushered in changes once thought to be exclusive to the giants of the commercial landscape. Let's dispel a myth: AI isn't a luxury reserved for Silicon Valley's elite; it's a toolkit ready to empower your business. With the advent of AI, local businesses have a suite of technological solutions capable of catalyzing growth and driving efficiency. Chatbots and predictive analytics––tools once sequestered within the confines of corporate juggernauts––are now accessible and, more impressively, adaptable to the smaller scales and niche needs of local commerce.

Imagine a tool that improves customer engagement without expanding your staff or an algorithm that anticipates supply needs before you're out of stock. These are not just pipe dreams; they're realities already within reach, thanks to localized AI applications. Consider the 4th Generation Communication LLC case, where implementing a savvy AI chatbot has revolutionized the customer service experience. Without adding to employee hours, they've slashed wait times and propelled customer satisfaction to new heights, illustrating a tangible transition from AI's potential to its profitable application.

In a landscape where every dollar counts, learning the contours of AI solutions aligns with cost-effective strategies, operational streamlining, and bolstered bottom lines. **AI has transformed from a buzzword into a bona fide business ally**, unlocking efficiencies and providing predictive insights that guide inventory management, deliver personalized customer experiences, and renovate marketing endeavors—all without supplanting the human touch that distinguishes local businesses.

Reluctance to embrace AI often stems from misconceptions about its complexity and reach. However, this chapter dissects the accessible nature of AI tools strategically designed for businesses that don't boast a sprawling workforce or an endless budget. **Discover that the AI revolution is not a tomorrow possibility but a today reality** for local businesses poised to ride the crest of this technological wave.

Pioneering Profit through Predictive Precision

As we delve into the specifics, it's integral to understand that implementing AI is not a gamble; it's a calculated enhancement meant to synergize with your current operations. To measure the success of AI integration, we should adopt a systematic approach that ensures our investments are not just wise but also profitable.

The Metric Method: Blueprinting Success in AI Deployment

Step 1: Define Key Metrics

Your first action is to establish the metrics that matter. These are the litmus tests for your AI's effectiveness in operational cost saving, efficiency, and customer satisfaction. For instance, you could measure the conversion rate uplift from a chatbot or the reduction in waste from better inventory predictions.

Step 2: Collect and Analyze Data

Then, gather data diligently––it's the lifeblood of decision-making. Comparison of pre and post-AI implementation data offers an evidentiary basis for your AI's impact. The insights gleaned here will serve as guideposts for adapting your strategies.

Step 3: Evaluate the ROI

With your data in hand, calculate the return on your investment. Assess not only the tangible gains but also the intangible ones, such as boosting your team's morale or enriching customer relationships, which can often transcend mere financial computation.

Step 4: Gather Feedback

No number speaks as clearly as human feedback. Poll your customers and interview your staff. This qualitative data is the soul amidst the spreadsheet cells––it can pivot your AI tactics toward even greater success.

Step 5: Adjust and Improve

Finally, it is *perfect through iteration*. Use the collected insights to fine-tune your AI, optimizing it to serve your business goals. It's an ongoing process, as the AI landscape is ever-evolving, and so should your tactics.

This step-by-step process isn't set in stone; it's meant to be a foundation upon which you can build and customize based on the needs and aspirations of your business. AI is the tool, local businesses are the craftsperson, and the resulting innovation is a masterpiece waiting to be revealed.

The myth that AI solutions are exclusively designed for large corporations with deep pockets and extensive resources has been shattered in today's fast-paced business landscape. Small and medium-sized enterprises can now access AI tools tailored specifically to their needs and resources. These AI solutions, ranging from chatbots for customer service to predictive analytics for inventory management, are not only accessible but also align perfectly with the goals and capabilities of local businesses.

Contrary to the belief that AI is out of reach for small enterprises, many have successfully leveraged AI to achieve cost savings, streamline operations, and boost profits. For instance, consider the case of a local auto repair shop that integrated an AI-powered system to streamline appointment scheduling and customer inquiries. The results were impressive, with a significant reduction in administrative tasks, allowing the business to focus more on servicing vehicles and providing a better customer experience. **AI brought about a tangible return on investment, enhancing the business's efficiency and bottom line.**

Another example is a boutique retail store that utilized AI-powered predictive analytics to optimize inventory management. The store maintained an ideal stock level by analyzing past sales data and predicting future trends, minimizing overstock and stockouts. As a result, the store saved costs on excess inventory and increased sales by having the right products available when customers wanted them. **The implementation of AI directly contributed to the business's success and growth.**

One company that stands out for providing tailored AI solutions for local businesses is 4th Generation Communication LLC. Through AI chatbots, businesses can streamline customer service, improve response times, and gather valuable insights about customer preferences and behaviors. For instance, a local bakery used 4th Generation Communication LLC's AI chatbot to handle customer orders, provide recommendations, and collect feedback on new products. The bakery saw a significant increase in customer satisfaction and loyalty, boosting sales and revenue. The AI chatbot improved customer engagement and allowed the bakery to focus on enhancing the quality of its products and services. **The implementation of AI had a direct and positive impact on the bakery's business.**

These success stories are just the beginning of the transformative power of AI for local businesses. Keep reading to understand how AI solutions like chatbots and predictive analytics are accessible and aligned with the goals of small enterprises.

In the age of digital transformation, artificial intelligence is not just a tool for large corporations; it holds significant potential for small and medium-sized local businesses. Tailored AI solutions, such as chatbots for customer service and predictive analytics for inventory management, are accessible and can align with the goals and resources of small enterprises. This availability demystifies the belief that AI is only for businesses with extensive resources and technical expertise. Small companies have successfully leveraged AI to achieve a positive return on investment, demonstrating the tangible benefits and accessibility of these solutions.

A compelling case study is 4th Generation Communication LLC, a small local business that implemented an AI chatbot to streamline its customer service operations. The chatbot, integrated with the company's website and social media platforms, efficiently handled customer inquiries, provided product information, and even assisted in processing orders. The AI chatbot drastically reduced the time and resources required for customer service, allowing the business to reallocate its human resources to more critical tasks. Additionally, the chatbot's 24/7 availability significantly enhanced the customer experience, increasing satisfaction and retention rates.

Another noteworthy example is a local retailer that utilized AI-powered predictive analytics for inventory management. By analyzing historical sales data, market trends, and seasonal variations, the predictive analytics solution enabled the retailer to optimize inventory levels, reduce carrying costs, and minimize stockouts. As a result, the business experienced a significant improvement in its supply chain efficiency, leading to cost savings and improved profitability. The seamless integration of AI into the retailer's operations illustrates how accessible and practical AI solutions can directly align with local businesses' unique needs and goals.

4th Generation Communication LLC's AI chatbot is a prime example of how small businesses can leverage AI to enhance efficiency, productivity, and customer satisfaction. The chatbot's ability to handle customer inquiries, provide real-time assistance, and facilitate seamless interactions exemplifies the transformative impact of accessible AI solutions. Moreover, the performance and success of this implementation stand as a testament to the practicality and relevance of AI for local businesses seeking to elevate their operations and deliver exceptional customer experiences.

By embracing tailored AI solutions like chatbots and predictive analytics, local businesses can unlock new levels of efficiency, productivity, and customer satisfaction. These accessible AI tools provide tangible benefits for small enterprises, offering a clear path to achieving a positive return on investment. The success stories of businesses that have harnessed the power of AI serve as compelling evidence of the potential value and impact awaiting those who embrace these innovative solutions. Through the strategic utilization of AI, small businesses can bolster their competitive edge, drive growth, and establish themselves as industry leaders in their respective markets.

The notion that sophisticated technologies like AI are exclusively in the realm of big tech companies is a common misconception. However, artificial intelligence is becoming increasingly relevant and accessible to smaller local businesses. With **tailored AI solutions**, these businesses are beginning to reap benefits such as increased efficiency, improved customer experience, and smarter decision-making processes. These solutions level the playing field, allowing small to medium businesses to compete head-to-head with larger corporations.

One illustrative example is the leap in customer service capabilities through AI chatbots, such as those offered by

4th Generation Communication LLC. These AI-driven systems can **handle customer inquiries** 24/7, without the need for breaks, and provide instant responses. A local bookstore, for instance, installed a chatbot that offered book recommendations and handled reservations, which led to improved customer satisfaction and a notable increase in sales, especially after hours when staff were not available to respond.

Investing in predictive analytics is another way AI empowers local businesses. For instance, a family-owned restaurant used AI to analyze its sales data and predict future inventory needs. This **predictive insight** prevented overstocking and food waste, optimized their menu offerings based on customer preferences, and delivered a positive return on investment by significantly reducing costs.

Moreover, AI solutions are customizable to a business's specific requirements. A boutique clothing store dealing with complex inventory and changing fashion trends implemented an AI system to monitor purchasing patterns. This tool refined their stock levels and offered actionable insights into trending products, resulting in a more agile response to market shifts.

AI solutions do more than automate - they **provide invaluable analytics** and insights that could take human employees much longer to compile and interpret. For instance, a local DIY hardware store implemented AI to track customer purchase behavior, leading to a tailored marketing strategy that boosted sales in targeted categories by 15%.

These stories underscore an important shift: **AI technology is tangible and actionable for local businesses**. AI tools bring significant value by automating routine tasks, providing data-driven insights, and enhancing customer engagement. This transformation is not reserved for the future—it is happening now, and local businesses are already reaping the rewards.

The **AI** requires a limited amount of resources and technical expertise as once thought. Many AI service providers cater to the needs of small businesses with scalable solutions and user-friendly interfaces. They also often offer supportive customer service to guide business owners through adoption. These aspects make AI tools not just accessible but also practical for a small business's operational scope.

Through AI chatbots, businesses can streamline customer service, improve response times, and gather valuable insights about customer preferences and behaviors **democratizing business access**, and empowering small and medium-sized enterprises to innovate, optimize, and flourish. Local businesses embracing these technologies position themselves to meet shifting market demands, gaining a competitive advantage usually seen in large corporations. This path could redefine success for small businesses in the digital age.

In today's business landscape, small and medium-sized enterprises leverage **AI solutions** to compete and thrive in their respective industries. The prevalent belief that AI is exclusively for large corporations with substantial resources is being systematically dispelled by the increasing availability of AI **tools** and **solutions** tailored to local businesses' unique needs and resources.

By understanding the accessibility and alignment of AI solutions like chatbots and predictive analytics with the goals of local businesses, entrepreneurs are discovering a pathway to unprecedented cost savings, increased profits, and market domination. For instance, consider the case of Mary's Boutique, a small local clothing store with a limited staff. By implementing a customer service chatbot, Mary's Boutique was able to provide quick and efficient responses to customer inquiries, resulting in a 30% increase in customer satisfaction and a significant reduction in labor costs.

Similarly, 4th Generation Communication LLC's AI chatbot has been instrumental in enhancing the customer experience for local businesses. Through natural language processing and machine learning, 4th Generation Communication LLC's chatbot has improved customer engagement and generated valuable insights about customer preferences and behavior. This has enabled businesses to tailor their marketing strategies, substantially increasing customer retention and loyalty. In one notable case, a local restaurant implemented the AI chatbot and saw a 40% increase in repeat customers, ultimately leading to a positive return on investment within three months.

It isn't just about profitability; AI solutions can also streamline operations and optimize resources. Take, for example, the experience of a local hardware store that integrated predictive analytics into its inventory management system. The store reduced carrying costs by accurately forecasting demand and optimizing stock levels, ensuring that popular products were always available. This increased customer satisfaction and freed up capital that could be reinvested in the business.

The stories of small businesses successfully implementing AI solutions underscore the transformative power of accessible AI tools. As you explore the potential for AI in your own business, consider how tailored solutions like chatbots and predictive analytics can revolutionize your operations and propel your business forward. Accessible AI is not just a luxury for the corporate giants; it's a practical and achievable advantage that can elevate your local business to new heights of success.

Chapter 9
Enhancing Human Productivity with AI

Amid the soft hum of servers and the rhythmic tapping of keyboards, Jenna, the operations manager at 4th Generation Communication LLC, leaned back in her chair and savored a rare moment of calm. Her office, with its walls adorned with flow charts and project timelines, had become a sanctuary where innovation blended seamlessly with efficiency. The recent integration of their AI chatbot had transformed the business, creating ripples of change that Jenna was still coming to terms with.

She remembered the skepticism that had clouded her thoughts when the idea was first pitched. AI—those two letters seemed to carry the weight of a promise or a threat, depending on whom you asked. Jenna had watched peers in other companies grapple with the balance of machines and man; too often, she saw technology cast as a usurper of roles rather than a partner. Yet, here she was, witnessing a silent revolution unfurl within her domain.

It was a client from six months back that lingered in her mind. Like many others, they served, a small business owner sought a means to bridge the gap between human fallibility and the uncompromising pace of customer demands. The solution came in the form of their AI chatbot, which had not only lifted the load from the customer service team's shoulders but had also sparked unforeseen creativity amongst them. Jenna recalled the faces of her employees as they engaged more with strategy and less with the mundane—the AI doing what it did best so the humans could do what only they could do.

Her thoughts were interrupted by the fragrance of coffee that drifted from the break room, signaling the late afternoon lull. Jenna took this cue to stroll between the cubicles, where the murmur of collaboration was a harmonious undertone. She paused by Mark, whose role had evolved from customer queries to customer experience strategist. There was an enthusiasm in his demeanor that Jenna had not seen when he was tethered to repetitive tasks.

"Jenna," he greeted her with reverence and familiarity, "we're testing a new interactive feature on the AI, one that integrates personalized recommendations for clients. It's fascinating how it learns and adapts."

"That's exactly the kind of innovation we're aiming for." Jenna's response was not just superficial but laced with genuine pride. The AI chatbot wasn't just a solution but a catalyst, propelling them toward a future where human ingenuity wasn't suppressed but augmented.

In her mind, Jenna ran through case studies she had read that quantified the positive ROI of AI implementation in small businesses. The chatbot had increased customer satisfaction and improved employee morale, resulting in a compound return that was more than just financial.

Late evening spread its orange glow through the office windows as Jenna returned to her desk. The balance sheets on her screen glowed, showing favorable numbers, a testament to the symbiosis of AI and human effort. As she prepared to shut down for the day, Jenna pondered the transformation within the walls of 4th Generation Communication LLC. This transformation was less about the technology itself and more about the people it served and the potential it unlocked.

Could the age of AI be less of an eclipse of human roles and more of a dawn for human potential?

Unleashing the Synergy of AI and Human Ingenuity

Artificial Intelligence is not a futuristic fantasy aimed at usurping human roles; it's a present-day reality designed to amplify human capabilities, especially in business. AI is a powerful ally for local businesses looking to stay relevant in a rapidly evolving market. The promise of AI lies in its ability to perform repetitive and mundane tasks, freeing up human workers to engage in work that requires a human touch—critical thinking, creative problem-solving, and personal customer interactions that truly define a brand.

By offloading these rote responsibilities to AI systems, businesses can expect a surge in overall efficiency and productivity. Humans can then apply their unique skills where they matter most, leveraging insights from AI to make data-driven decisions and drive innovation. Implementing AI does not equate to job displacement but to job enhancement, enabling employees to maximize their potential and satisfaction in the workplace.

Understanding the transformative power of AI is critical. In the realm of small and local businesses, the application of AI can be the catalyst for unprecedented growth and profitability. For instance, AI can manage inventory, predict customer preferences, and streamline operations, all while providing actionable data that can inform strategic decisions. This application of technology propels businesses ahead, enabling them to excel in competitive markets without succumbing to overwhelm.

Case studies in the small business arena are a testament to the tangible ROI that AI can deliver. Consider a local bookshop employing machine learning algorithms to predict which genres sell best each season. The result? Higher sales, reduced overstock, and delighted customers. AI is not just for the tech giants; it's accessible and game-changing for businesses of any scale.

One compelling story emerges from 4th Generation Communication LLC, where an AI chatbot revolutionized customer service. *With this AI-driven interface, response times plummeted, customer satisfaction shot up, and employees were redeployed to more strategic roles.* Such stories illustrate that AI is not a competitor but a collaborator, vital to constructing a more resilient and successful business.

As we delve deeper into this technological synergy, it becomes clear that AI's role is not to make humans redundant but to augment their skills and contributions. Embracing AI means cultivating a more engaged and contented workforce, where creativity and strategic thinking become the day-to-day rather than an afterthought. The potential for AI to impact businesses positively is undeniable, and it's an opportunity for local businesses to survive and thrive.

The journey to AI implementation should be strategic and mindful, avoiding a one-size-fits-all approach. Tailoring AI to the specific needs of a business ensures that its introduction is smooth and its impact, profound. As we progress through this exploration, remember that the essence of AI in business is to harness its strengths to embellish, not eclipse, human proficiency—a partnership leading to collective prosperity and advancement.

Regarding AI implementation, the primary aim is to enhance human productivity rather than replace human workers entirely. This approach acknowledges the unique capabilities and value that human employees bring to the table while leveraging AI to streamline and optimize routine tasks. By reallocating repetitive and mundane responsibilities to AI systems, businesses can empower their human workforce to focus on more strategic and creative duties, driving innovation and growth. This shift leads to a more engaged and fulfilled workforce and fosters a culture of continuous improvement and adaptability.

AI has demonstrated its capacity to enhance human productivity in various industries, including small businesses. For instance, consider the case of a local retail store that integrated AI-powered inventory management systems. By automating inventory tracking and restocking processes, the employees could devote more time to customer service, product merchandising, and market analysis. This led to a significant improvement in customer satisfaction, sales efficiency, and overall business performance. The AI system didn't replace the employees but complemented their efforts and contributed to their success.

Similarly, a small marketing agency implemented AI-driven data analytics tools to process and interpret the vast amounts of consumer data. This allowed the marketing team to gain deeper insights into customer behavior, preferences, and market trends, enabling them to devise more targeted and impactful marketing campaigns. As a result, the business experienced increased client retention rates and expanded its customer base while empowering the employees to harness their creativity and strategic thinking.

One compelling example is the telecommunications industry, where 4th Generation Communication LLC deployed an AI chatbot to handle customer inquiries and support requests. As a result, the employees serving in customer support roles could reallocate their time and skills to focus on complex customer issues and strategic planning, ultimately boosting customer satisfaction and loyalty. This innovative use of AI improved operational efficiency and elevated the overall quality of the customer experience, illustrating how AI can enhance human productivity rather than supplant it.

The essence of AI implementation lies in leveraging technology to amplify human potential, not diminish it. Businesses can foster a culture of innovation and advancement by allowing employees to channel their expertise and creativity into more meaningful endeavors. This approach benefits the workforce and contributes to the business's success and longevity. The next section will delve into the beneficial impact of reallocating routine tasks to AI systems, uncovering the opportunities it creates for strategic and creative growth.

AI implementation can transform businesses' operations, offering many benefits while streamlining processes, maximizing efficiency, and enhancing productivity. One prominent advantage of reallocating routine tasks to AI systems is the potential to empower human employees to focus on strategic and creative responsibilities. By effectively leveraging AI technology, small business owners can cultivate a more engaged and fulfilled workforce, driving overall business success.

Let's dive into a real-life case study of how 4th Generation Communication LLC implemented an AI chatbot to improve customer service and productivity. This small business, specializing in digital marketing services, utilized an AI chatbot to field basic customer inquiries, schedule appointments, and provide initial assistance. By reallocating these routine customer service tasks to the AI chatbot, human employees could allocate more time towards developing personalized marketing strategies for their clients. As a result, the efficiency of the business was greatly enhanced, enabling the team to handle a higher volume of clients while delivering exceptional quality work. This led to increased client satisfaction and allowed 4th Generation Communication LLC to expand its client base and achieve a positive return on investment (ROI) by implementing AI technology.

The benefits of reallocating routine tasks to AI systems extend beyond customer service and can be applied to various operational aspects of a business. For instance, small businesses can streamline data entry, reporting, and administrative processes by leveraging AI-driven automation tools. This frees up valuable time for employees to focus on more critical decision-making, strategic planning, and creative problem-solving. Consequently, businesses can innovate more rapidly, adapt to market changes, and maintain a competitive edge in their industry.

In another case study, a local e-commerce store utilized AI-powered inventory management systems to automate stock monitoring, reorder processes, and demand forecasting. By reallocating these routine inventory management tasks to AI systems, human employees could concentrate on developing targeted marketing campaigns, optimizing the customer experience, and identifying new product lines. As a result, the e-commerce store experienced a significant increase in sales, reduced operational costs, and improved customer satisfaction. This example further demonstrates the potential for AI implementation to enhance human productivity and drive business growth.

The strategic reallocation of repetitive tasks to AI systems increases human productivity and fosters a more engaged and fulfilled workforce. A study conducted by a team of researchers from leading universities found that employees relieved of repetitive, mundane tasks due to AI implementation reported higher job satisfaction, increased motivation, and a greater sense of purpose in their work. This shift in responsibilities allowed employees to tap into their full potential, exercise creativity, and contribute meaningfully to the business's overall success.

Fostering a work environment where human employees are empowered to focus on strategic and creative responsibilities can lead to a culture of innovation and continuous improvement. Businesses that effectively utilize AI to reallocate routine tasks can create teams that are more resilient, adaptable, and capable of driving innovation to propel the company forward.

The benefits of reallocating routine tasks to AI systems are manifold, enhancing human productivity and contributing to a more engaged and fulfilled workforce. By empowering human employees to focus on strategic and creative responsibilities, businesses can cultivate a culture of innovation, adaptability, and enhanced performance, driving overall business success. The strategic integration of AI technology lays the foundation for businesses to thrive in the digital age, maximizing their potential for growth and market domination.

The Human-AI Synergy

When implemented thoughtfully, Artificial Intelligence complements the workforce like a skilled ensemble, enhancing the rhythm of productivity and creativity. One of the most significant changes AI brings is the freeing up of employees' time from monotonous tasks, **redirecting their focus towards works that matter**—strategy, innovation, and direct customer relations. These are areas where human judgment and emotional intelligence irreplaceably shine. By entrusting AI with routine workflows, businesses experience a surge in efficiency and foster a culture where employees are more engaged and invested in outcomes, seeing their efforts align closely with core business objectives.

The Creative Rebirth

In the realm of small businesses, the adoption of AI can feel like a **renaissance of resourcefulness**. With intelligent systems in place, employees are now liberated to engage in creative problem-solving, contributing ideas for new products, services, or processes that could revolutionize the market. For instance, a boutique marketing firm employed AI tools for data analysis and campaign adjustments, previously consuming the bulk of their time. This shift allowed their creative team to double down on storytelling and personalized content strategies, translating to a dramatic uptick in client engagement and satisfaction.

Empowerment Through AI

Leveraging AI can directly translate into the empowerment of the workforce. A case in point is a local retail chain's adoption of 4th Generation Communication LLC's AI chatbot. This technology improved customer service and empowered sales staff with real-time inventory data and consumer insights. With a **solid digital assistant** at their side, the staff was able to provide personalized shopping experiences, resulting in increased customer loyalty and a visible growth in sales.

AI's Role in Delighting Customers

AI and human innovation can elevate customer experiences to unprecedented heights. Consider a family-owned restaurant that integrated AI to manage reservations and ordering processes. This allowed the staff to refocus on customer interactions and service quality. As a result, the restaurant saw a significant increase in repeat business, driven by customers' appreciation for the attentive service and personal touch—a crucial differentiator in the hospitality industry.

Strategic Human-AI Allocation

The efficiency gained from AI is best realized when businesses strategically align their human capital with AI capabilities. A local hardware store capitalized on this by employing AI for inventory management and predictive ordering. This freed employees from back-office tasks, allowing them to engage with customers and provide expert project advice. Customers valued the hands-on guidance, and employees found greater satisfaction in their roles, knowing they were making a meaningful impact on customer experiences.

The Morale Factor

Introducing AI can lead to an unexpected boon: a boost in employee morale. Ensuring that AI tools handle menial tasks efficiently helps build a workplace environment where **innovation is rewarded, and burnout is reduced**. A graphic design studio experienced this firsthand when they used AI to streamline administrative tasks and workflow management. The designers had more time to dedicate to their creative passions, leading to a portfolio of more ambitious and higher-quality work that attracted bigger clients and propelled the studio's reputation.

Driving Business Success with AI

AI's impact on business success isn't just theoretical—it's demonstrably substantial. An online retailer's use of machine learning for personalized recommendations resulted in an impressive increase in average order value and customer retention rates. By providing employees with deep customer insights, they could tailor experiences and offers, making every interaction count. This enhanced the company's bottom line and created a **shared sense of accomplishment** among the team, reinforcing the collective drive towards business objectives.

The Long-Term Impact

The elevated human productivity facilitated by AI doesn't just provide immediate gains—it also sets the stage for long-term success. Businesses embracing AI to augment their workforce report lower turnover rates, as employees are more likely to stay with an organization that invests in their growth and values their contributions. This investment in human capital is recognized as a decisive factor in building a resilient and adaptable business capable of weathering market fluctuations and technological advancements.

These narratives show that the union of AI and human potential generates a hub for growth, engagement, and productivity. As AI assumes the routinized tasks, it catalyzes a shift where human creativity and strategic thinking become the driving forces behind successful business ventures. Far from the cold robotic takeover imagined in dystopian narratives, *AI in practice proves to be a harbinger of a more human-centric workplace*, emphasizing the value of each individual's contribution to the collective success of a business.

In the modern business landscape, integrating AI has proven to enhance human productivity rather than replace it. By reallocating routine tasks to AI systems, businesses can empower their human employees to focus on strategic and creative responsibilities, ultimately driving higher levels of innovation, problem-solving, and customer engagement. This shift not only leads to a more engaged and fulfilled workforce but also has the potential to impact the bottom line significantly.

Consider the case of a local retail store that implemented AI-powered inventory management systems. By automating restocking and supply chain optimization, they freed up their employees from mundane data entry and inventory tracking tasks. This allowed the staff to dedicate their time to understanding customer preferences, designing unique promotions, and creating personalized shopping experiences. As a result, the store saw a significant increase in customer satisfaction, repeat business, and an uptick in revenue.

Similarly, 4th Generation Communication LLC's AI chatbot solution has transformed how small businesses engage with customers. The chatbot has streamlined customer service through personalized interactions, instant responses, and predictive analytics and unearthed valuable insights into consumer preferences and pain points. This has allowed businesses to tailor their offerings, marketing strategies, and product development to meet customer needs better, ultimately leading to a positive return on investment.

The key takeaway is that AI implementation is not about replacing humans with machines; it's about leveraging technology to elevate human potential and drive business success. By embracing AI to tackle the repetitive and mundane, businesses can unleash their employees' creativity, problem-solving skills, and strategic thinking, ultimately propelling the organization forward.

As we move into the next chapter, we will explore how AI can lead to tangible cost savings, increased profits, and market domination for local businesses. But before that, it's essential to recognize the paradigm shift AI brings to the human workforce and how this can be leveraged for the greater good of the business and the community it serves.

Chapter 10
Ethical Considerations in AI Implementation

Amid the soft hum of computers and the faint scent of freshly brewed coffee, Jenna sat at her desk, her eyes fixed on the screen, navigating through the sea of sensitive customer data. The weight of responsibility sat heavily on her shoulders in the quaint office of 4th Generation Communication LLC, a modest tech company in the heart of the bustling city. Ensuring privacy and data security in the company's AI implementation was not just a task—a promise, a vow taken to protect the very essence of the people who trusted them.

A notification popped up on her screen—a gentle reminder of a scheduled meeting with a small business client whose fortunes had turned favorably after adopting their latest AI chatbot. This success story, a case study now, harbored the trust cultivated through transparency among its lines. Months back, apprehensive and guarded, the client had deliberated their decision until Jenna's team presented the project with the fidelity of an open book—adherence to data protection regulations and the non-negotiables of customer relations.

Outside, the melody of the bustling city was punctuated by the regular chimes of the nearby clock tower—striking the hour, bringing her back from her reverie. The office's plant-lined windows let in dapples of sunlight, playing across the hardwood floor, a daily performance unnoticed by many but comforting in its reliability.

Jenna's colleague, Michael, emerged from his office, briefcase in hand, ready for the day's external consulting sessions. "Are we good on that security update?" he asked, pausing by her desk. "Running as of 8 AM," she replied without lifting her gaze. "You know, it's more than just the code. It's about the peace people feel when interacting with our systems," he added thoughtfully. Jenna nodded, the weight of their shared responsibility mirrored in her colleague's solemn tone.

As she observed Michael head out, the reflections on ethical and responsible AI adoption settled within her. It was about planting seeds for long-term customer relationships, for the brand loyalty that thrives in the soil of trust and care.

Jenna stood up, stretching from the long hours of attention paid to her screen, and walked to the large bay window. The city, a mosaic of life and stories, seemed close yet distant from this vantage point. As her fingertips traced the cool glass, she wondered how many more businesses could bloom by integrating their AI chatbot and how many more lives could be touched by the invisible thread of ethical AI.

Reflecting on the road ahead, she considered the profound question that lingered in the minds of all those who tread this path: If trust is the currency of today's digital economy, how do we ensure our AI implementations not only spend it wisely but also contribute to its growth?

The Unseen Backbone of AI: Ethics at the Core

Welcome to the pivotal juncture where technology meets morality. As you delve into AI, a nagging question looms: Are you handling your newfound capabilities responsibly? AI can be a transformative force for your local business, but as we've learned, it's not merely about harnessing this power but about wielding it with integrity. To sustain the momentum gathered from AI's cost savings and market advantages, one must grapple with the ethical implications of AI integration. Data privacy and security are not merely checkboxes for compliance; they stand as pillars of trust in the foundation of your customer relationships.

Data is the lifeblood of modern business, yet with great data collection comes great responsibility. Ensuring privacy in AI systems is strategically important, requiring a keen understanding of legal obligations and ethical imperatives. Neglect in this domain can lead to severe repercussions, not just legally, but in the erosion of customer trust that can be devastating for any local business aiming to make a mark. As this chapter unfolds, we will delve deep into privacy's linchpin role and why it should never be an afterthought in your AI strategy.

Transparency is more than a buzzword; it's a crucial component of a sustainable AI strategy. Adherence to data protection regulations is not just about obedience to laws; it demonstrates your commitment to your customers' rights. By exploring the intricate dance between regulatory compliance and openness, we find that a transparent approach culminates in a robust relationship with the customer, where trust is the unwavering constant.

Choosing the path of ethical and responsible AI adoption isn't merely a moral obligation; it's a strategic business move. *Long-term customer relationships and brand loyalty are the lifeblood of local businesses*, and they can only be nurtured when customers feel valued and respected. This chapter will highlight how ethical practices in AI serve as the cornerstone of enduring customer loyalty and, ultimately, business success. We'll weave in case studies illustrating the tangible benefits that businesses have reaped by putting ethics at the forefront of their AI endeavors.

Within these pages, you will learn from businesses that have become case studies in AI ethics done right. For instance, a small retailer leveraged AI to personalize shopping experiences without compromising customer data security, earning profits and customers' lifelong trust. Or how 4th Generation Communication LLC's AI chatbot became more than a technological tool—it transformed into an ambassador of the company's ethical standards, endearing the company to users while solving their queries efficiently.

As we conclude the book, reflecting on our journey from AI novices to informed practitioners, we realize that *ethics is not a destination but a continuous journey*. It brings together all we have learned: the mechanics of AI, the insights into market trends, the innovative strategies for staying competitive, and the profound understanding that in AI, as in all business ventures, how we achieve success is just as important as the success itself.

Building Trust Through Data Security and Respect for Privacy

Let's envisage a future where your business thrives in competitive markets while upholding the highest ethical standards in AI. This future is not a pipedream but a roadmap in the chapters we traversed. The final layer we add is the sheath of ethics—where AI does not overshadow human values but is made subservient to them. By the end of this chapter, you will not only appreciate the generosity of ethical AI but will be equipped to implement it in a way that solidifies your business as a bastion of trust and innovation.

As businesses delve into the world of AI implementation, ensuring privacy and data security is of paramount importance. With the collection and analysis of vast amounts of customer data, protecting this information becomes a critical ethical consideration. **Businesses**

must prioritize the confidentiality and security of customer data, fostering trust and loyalty.

Consider the case of a small retail business that integrated AI into its customer relationship management system. The business could personalize marketing efforts and improve product recommendations by analyzing customer data. However, to ensure ethical AI implementation, it was crucial to prioritize data security and privacy. By doing so, the business gained valuable insights from customer data and built trust with its clientele, fostering long-term relationships and brand loyalty.

It's essential to recognize that in the age of AI, customer data can be leveraged to enhance personalization and customer experience. Still, it also requires a deep commitment to the ethical handling of data. **Transparency and adherence to data protection regulations are key factors in building trust with customers.** Small businesses can learn from this, realizing that transparency in data usage and a commitment to regulations can be the cornerstone of ethical AI implementation.

One notable illustration of this principle in action is the story of a local law firm that leveraged AI to improve efficiency in document review processes. The firm was vigilant in ensuring the privacy and security of sensitive legal information, reinforcing its commitment to ethical AI adoption. This commitment translated into trust from both existing and potential clients, further solidifying the firm's reputation and brand loyalty.

Thus, **ethical and responsible AI adoption isn't just a moral imperative; it also plays a vital role in establishing long-term customer relationships and brand loyalty.** By prioritizing the ethical use of AI, businesses can ensure that their customers feel secure in their interactions, leading to sustained patronage and advocacy. In striving for ethical AI adoption, businesses commit to accountability and goodwill, fostering a business environment rooted in integrity and respect.

Dive deeper into the ethical considerations surrounding AI implementation and understand how prioritizing privacy and data security is crucial for building customer trust in the next section.

In AI implementation, transparency and adherence to data protection regulations are pivotal in building customer trust. In today's data-driven world, customers are increasingly aware of the value and sensitivity of their personal information. As a result, businesses prioritizing transparency and compliance with data protection regulations stand to earn customer trust and loyalty. In this section, we'll explore the significance of these factors and their impact on businesses adopting AI.

Case studies present compelling evidence that small businesses have achieved a positive return on investment (ROI) by embracing AI. By examining real-world examples, we can understand the tangible benefits that transparency and adherence to data protection regulations can offer. Small businesses that have effectively utilized AI to safeguard customer data have seen increased customer trust and loyalty, ultimately improving business performance.

In the age of AI, customer trust is paramount. Businesses that fail to prioritize transparency and compliance with data protection regulations risk losing the trust of their customer base. As such, it is imperative for businesses to **embrace transparency** and communicate openly with their customers about how their data is being used and protected. This transparency not only fosters trust but also positions the business as ethical and responsible in the eyes of its customers.

One standout example is 4th Generation Communication LLC's AI chatbot, which has helped numerous businesses improve customer engagement and data security simultaneously. By leveraging AI, businesses can enhance customer experiences while maintaining robust data protection measures. Through the stories of businesses that have integrated 4th Generation Communication LLC's AI chatbot, we can see how transparency and adherence to data protection regulations have contributed to their success.

When businesses prioritize transparency and compliance with data protection regulations, they build trust with their customers and establish themselves as ethical and responsible AI adopters. This, in turn, contributes to long-term customer relationships and brand loyalty. By weaving ethical considerations into their AI implementation strategies, businesses can position themselves for sustainable success in an increasingly data-conscious marketplace.

In summary, transparency and adherence to data protection regulations in AI implementation are undeniably crucial. Small businesses that embrace these principles can effectively build trust with their customer base, paving the way for long-term success and brand loyalty. Through case studies and real-world examples, we can see how businesses have reaped the benefits of prioritizing transparency and data protection, ultimately boosting their performance and customer relationships.

The Cornerstone of Customer Loyalty

Customer trust and loyalty are not just buzzwords but the foundation of a prosperous business venture in the digital age. Ethical and responsible AI adoption underscores a commitment to these values. Business owners who integrate AI into their operations must focus on the efficiency it delivers and the trust it can foster or break. When customers see that a business prioritizes their privacy and safety, they anchor their loyalty in its responsible practices. For instance, when a retail store employs a customer service AI that securely manages transaction records, customers are reassured about their data security, enhancing their trust in the brand.

Practical Benefits of Ethical AI

The practical benefits of ethical AI stretch beyond customer satisfaction; they translate into tangible business value. A local insurance company incorporating AI to streamline claims processing while strictly adhering to ethical guidelines saw an impressive uptick in customer retention. This is not a mere coincidence. Customers feel more secure when they know their sensitive information is handled with integrity and care. Such an ethical stance protects the business from legal backlashes and positions the brand as a trustworthy entity that customers are happy to return to and recommend.

Investing in Trust

Investing in AI technology is investing in the future of your brand-customer relationship. When businesses consciously adopt AI solutions aligned with ethical standards, they invest in a bridge of trust with their clients. Let's take the example of 4th Generation Communication LLC's AI chatbot. Designed for engagement and responsiveness, the bot operates with a clear protocol to protect user data, earning customer goodwill as it facilitates seamless interactions. This commitment to ethical practice pays dividends in customer trust, a currency invaluable in the modern marketplace.

The Ripple Effect of Responsible AI

The broader impact of ethical AI on brand name and customer relationships cannot be overstated. Businesses that navigate the complexities of AI with a moral compass don't just influence their immediate customer base; they set an industry standard. Consider how a local grocery chain's use of AI in inventory management, with a firm stance on vendor data privacy, inspires the entire supply chain to uphold higher ethical practices. This ripple effect can revolutionize how businesses approach AI and client relationships in small and medium enterprise operations.

The Power of Transparency

Transparency in AI implementation acts as a beacon, guiding customers to trustworthy businesses. It is not enough to have an AI system in place; it is crucial to communicate how it works, its benefits, and its safeguards to the customer. For example, a local fitness center using AI for personalized workout recommendations can garner loyalty by clearly explaining how customer data informs these recommendations while ensuring absolute data protection. This transparency cements customer confidence and loyalty, as they appreciate the value without fearing for privacy.

Fostering Long-Term Relationships

In the long run, the businesses that stand the test of time establish and maintain ethical bonds with their clientele. Case in point: a small bookstore implementing an AI-driven recommendation system saw repeat customers because they transparently handled analytics and respected customer preferences. The AI allowed for a more personalized browsing experience, and the ethical handling of data ensured that customers felt understood and valued rather than just another sales target.

Brand Loyalty Through Ethical Practices

Brand loyalty flows from consistent and ethical engagement with customers. For small businesses, this means not just implementing AI for its cutting-edge benefits but doing so with a clear ethical framework. This principle was evident when a local coffee shop introduced an AI-based loyalty program that securely managed customer preferences and rewarded them accordingly. Customers loved the personalized attention, and knowing their data was secure, they frequented the shop more, boosting sales and its reputation.

AI stands out as a tool of infinite potential in a business landscape growing ever-reliant on technology. However, as small business owners harness this potential, they must also understand that the long-term success enabled by AI is tied to the responsible and ethical use of technology. *By prioritizing the ethical considerations as much as the strategic ones*, businesses meet the present-day demands and fortify their future in an AI-driven world.

In summary, **ethical considerations in AI implementation are non-negotiable for businesses**. It's imperative to prioritize privacy and data security in collecting and analyzing customer data. By adhering to data protection regulations and emphasizing transparency, businesses can build customer trust and solidify their reputation as ethical and responsible AI adopters, leading to long-term customer relationships and brand loyalty.

Throughout this book, we've delved into the intricacies of integrating AI into local businesses, demystifying the potential hurdles and showcasing the immense benefits. From cost reduction to profit optimization, the power of AI is palpable, and its impact is profound.

By embracing AI, businesses can streamline processes, understand customer behavior at a granular level, and enhance decision-making with actionable insights. The stories of businesses like Fourth Generation Communication LLC have demonstrated how AI has revolutionized their operations, leading to substantial returns on investment and propelling them ahead of the competition. The AI chatbot developed by Fourth Generation Communication LLC stands as a testament to the transformative power of AI, offering personalized experiences and driving unparalleled customer satisfaction.

As we close this chapter, remember that the journey to AI integration is a commitment to excellence and ethical responsibility. It's a dedication to embracing technological advancements for the betterment of your business, your customers, and the community at large. With the right knowledge and understanding, you have the potential to propel your local business to new heights, contribute to the greater good, and make a lasting impact in your industry.

So, as you embark on this AI journey, remember that ethical considerations are not just a choice but an obligation. Embrace the power of AI and wield it responsibly, and you will surely soar ahead in your market, equipped with newfound knowledge and understanding that set you apart as a visionary leader in your industry.

Unleashing the Power of AI: A Journey to Business Transformation

As we bring our exploration to a close, remember that the essence of this journey lies in harnessing the transformative power of artificial intelligence, turning it into a catalyst for growth, efficiency, and market leadership. Real-world applications of AI are no longer scenes from a science fiction movie; they are practical tools reshaping local business operations' foundations.

Implementing AI in your business may seem daunting, but armed with the insights from this book, the path ahead should now be clear. From understanding the potential cost savings to recognizing the pathways to increased profits and market domination, you know what is necessary to make AI work for you.

Recalling the core concepts, we revisited the significance of AI in streamlining operations, predictive analytics in enhancing decision-making, and chatbots like those from 4th Generation Communication LLC in revolutionizing customer service. Case studies within these pages illustrated tangible returns on investment, providing a blueprint for your success story.

To convert these ideas into actions, identify which AI applications are most relevant to your business. Then, develop a strategic plan to integrate these tools, considering short-term gains and long-term transformations. Remember to allocate resources wisely, opting for incremental change to alleviate overwhelm and allow your team to adapt seamlessly.

While this text offers comprehensive guidance, it is but a starting point. The rapid evolution of AI technologies requires continual **learning and adaptation**. Delve into ongoing research, attend industry conferences, and network with other entrepreneurs to stay ahead of the curve.

Now is the time to leap into action, leveraging AI's competitive advantage. Let this book be a source of knowledge and a springboard for innovation and change within your local business landscape.

Embrace the call to transform, knowing that every step towards AI integration positions your enterprise not only for survival but for unprecedented growth and influence.

In the spirit of constant improvement and contribution, remember that the implementation of AI transcends profit margins and efficiencies—it also holds the potential to contribute meaningfully to society, whether through enhanced services, new job opportunities, or supporting causes that align with your brand's values. Harnessing AI responsibly is as much about driving economic success as enhancing the greater good.

Let's conclude with a call to arms: **take the knowledge you've gathered, the strategies you've formed, and the inspiration you've cultivated** to embark on a transformative journey. The future of your business awaits, and it is bright with the promise of AI.

A Lasting Impression: Embrace the AI Revolution

May the final words of this book linger in your mind as a constant reminder that the future belongs to those brave enough to embrace change and bold enough to lead it. This is not the end of the road but the beginning of a thrilling adventure into the depth of what your business can truly achieve.

"For the best return on your money, pour your purse into your head." – **Benjamin Franklin**.

Through the diligent application of the knowledge shared here, may you pour the potential of AI into the heart of your business, and may your investment of time, effort, and innovation yield prosperity and a legacy of success.

Discover the Secrets to Implementing AI for Cost Savings, Increased Profits, and Market Domination Without being overwhelmed.